Discernment

Discernment

THE ART OF CHOOSING WELL

PIERRE WOLFF

LIGUORI/TRIUMPH
LIGUORI, MISSOURI

Published by Liguori/Triumph
An Imprint of Liguori Publications
Liguori, Missouri
http://www.liguori.org

Cover photo by Sandy Paton.

Library of Congress Cataloging-in-Publication Data

Wolff, Pierre
    Discernment / Pierre Wolff.
        p.   cm.
    Includes bibliographical reference and index.
    ISBN 0-89243-485-6
    1. Decision making—Religious aspects—Christianity. I. Title.
BV4509.2.W64   1993
248.4—dc20

                                                        93-7922

"Day by day, dear Lord,
of Thee three things I pray.
To see Thee more clearly,
Love Thee more dearly,
Follow Thee more nearly,
Day by day."

Richard of Chichester
c. 1197–1253

CONTENTS

INTRODUCTION

In our family, professional, social, and political life, we all —
believers or nonbelievers — face choices. If, in the past, we
have made some good choices that were beneficial for both
ourselves and for others, we have also, probably, made some
mistakes that did nobody any good. When we reflect, our fa-
milial, social, or political crises remind us that it is important to
be able to choose well.

One aspect of some of our worst choices may affect us
deeply. How often have we had the impression that our most
disastrous decisions were made under the influence of unconscious motivations. So, we followed passively either the counsel
of others or our own incontrollable impulse. We were led when
we thought we were choosing freely. Anyone who is addicted to
something or dependent on someone knows how painful it is
not to be in charge of one's decisions.

For people who have religious faith an important part of
what is at stake for them in their decisions is their companionship with God. Because of their belief, they desire to walk with
God. That requires them to avoid wandering away from the
One they worship, and they hope to make straight the highway
for God.(Is 40) As believers, they are concerned also about
finding out what God might want for them. And they desire to
act in accordance with what they discover so that they do not
lose the company of the One they serve. For Christians, looking
for God's presence and invitation in their daily life, the problem
of discernment was summarized by Andrew and his friend
when they asked Jesus the important question, "Master, where
do you live?" (Jn 1: 38)

So then, if we want to increase our chances of making fruitful choices for others and for ourselves, to manage our deci-

sions with greater freedom and to be faithful to our God, we need to learn to discern.

Discernment is the process of making choices that correspond as closely as possible to objective reality, that are as free as possible from our inner compulsions, and that are closely attuned to the convictions of our faith (or to our value system, if we have no religious belief).

The content of this book is an interpretation of a method of discernment that has stood the test of time in Christian tradition. In the sixteenth century, the founder of the Jesuits, Ignatius of Loyola, developed a systematic way of considering and making choices. This is the heritage that I would like to present, supported by my own years of experience in helping many people make choices.

Many articles and books have been written on this subject. Some of the books I have read are satisfactory to me. But some people have told me that they could not really get into them, because the technical language became an obstacle. Specialists in spiritual matters might find some parts of this essay too simple, but that has been precisely my purpose: to write a book that is at the same time *accurate but simple, complete but not too long, and understandable to everyone.*

This book is an introduction to discernment in the sense that it is going to be effective *only* if its content is put into practice. Discernment is not a theory, but a concrete way of dealing with daily reality that leads to making choices that affect our lives and the lives of others.

The content of the following pages is born from my own practice. I have led many directed retreats and workshops, and I have helped many individuals as well. The people I have met represent all levels of intellectual training, social and professional status, in several different countries. They were usually Christians, but I did work with people of non-Christian faiths and with nonbelievers. Therefore, I know this book can help *everybody* to use the ordinary tools we all have for making decisions, for *discerning.*

STRUCTURE OF THE BOOK

PART ONE shows that behind the sophisticated vocabulary of some specialists, discernment is based on abilities we all have. The framework, tools, and cornerstone are everybody's. The question is to learn how to use them methodically when it is time to make a decision.

PART TWO describes the method of discerning *for an individual person*. I start with the individual discernment before explaining the discernment of a group of people because I am deeply convinced by what I have seen that a body of people can't discern if its members are unable to discern personally.

First, I describe how to use the means at our disposal, head and heart. Even if the description uses Christian notions, a translation is possible for non-Christians or for nonbelievers. It is found in the Appendix entitled, *Is This Method Only For Christians?* Then, I go further to refine the method for use in cases that are more difficult to solve —for example, when a choice requires us to pass through an impulsive reaction that hides the deepest desire of our being. Finally, the description goes back to the basic requirement of any personal choice, *freedom*. How do we assure that it is a part of the process from the beginning?

PART THREE treats discernment that is made *by a group of people* (the temptation for some readers might be to go immediately to this part; I repeat what I have already said: such discernment requires that the members of a group know first how to discern personally).

In this part, I introduce a situation where an individual faced with making a personal choice asks a group for help in discerning. Then, I develop the case of the group reaching a common decision.

FINAL REFLECTIONS ON OUR DECISIONS reminds us of the last test and criterion concerning all our decisions: what we do for the poor. And eventually, we see what kind of salvation God wants for us in all our decisions.

At the end of the book, the reader will find some additional information that may be helpful. Appendix 1 details in a more complete way the four criteria for making a choice as explained in the book. Appendix 2 translates the method for use by people who are not Christians or not believers. Appendix 3 gives some suggestions for clarifying the object of the choice. Appendix 4 describes what to expect from a good spiritual helper. Finally, Appendix 5 includes four diagrams to help the reader present the steps of discernment in a visual fashion. Appendix 6 is an index of the Scripture passages referenced in this book. The quotations of the Bible I refer to are from *The Jerusalem Bible* and *The New American Bible* translations.

At this point I can make the reader a promise. If you learn and practice this method you will have the satisfaction of making better decisions, you will taste the joy of greater personal freedom; and, if you wish, you will experience the deep intimacy of deciding with your God. If you are not a believer, you will experience the contentment that comes when you are true to your most important values. I make this promise confidently, because those who followed the method evinced such contentment and serenity.

I would like to thank all the people through whom I learned how to discern. Some taught me, some helped me spiritually. Some shared their discernment with me, either as individuals or as groups. I would also like to thank those who have helped me to translate my ideas into a simple and understandable language. And a very special thank you to Carol.

Pierre Wolff
1992

Discernment

PART ONE

The Components of Any Choice

1

Everybody Has What Is Necessary for Choosing

The subject of discernment is currently in vogue. Although we hear the word used very frequently, the process remains mysterious for a lot of people. It might appear that its mastery is the privilege of certain spiritual or theological specialists such as ministers and priests, gurus and monks, and other experts. However, once discernment is explained, this is obviously not the case. Actually, everyone discerns since everyone makes choices, for life requires all of us to make daily decisions. And it is possible to do this in a more or less systematic way.

The verb *to discern* comes from the Latin verb *discernere*, which means to separate, to distinguish accurately one object from another. Discernment is a process that allows a person to see, without confusion and ambiguity, what differentiates things. It should be immediately obvious that this process is necessary for making a choice. Choosing requires discriminating. To choose the sidewalk, for example, is to choose not to walk on the street. But this simple choice presupposes that we are able to distinguish the sidewalk from the street—more clearly than, say, a drunken person whose sight and balance are disturbed by alcohol. The better our discernment, the clearer our choices.

We discern daily. Normally, it would be trivializing the word discernment if we were to apply it to selecting from a menu. However, if I am watching my cholesterol level, I need to take the time to decide what I am going to eat. First, I cross red meats, butter, and creamy cheeses off my list. Then, from the remaining options, I choose what I would prefer: veal or fish, raw or cooked vegetables, pasta, potatoes, or a bean dish. This opportunity for decision that recurs as regularly as our daily meals contains all the elements of the most systematic and sophisticated discernment. Holding aside for the moment any religious connotation of discernment, let us consider a few examples that may be more consequential than choosing a menu. For instance, let us suppose that we must move, find a new job, or choose a school for one of our children. What is the best way to approach such decisions?

THE FRAMEWORK: TIME

To the extent that the situation permits, we never want to make a decision in a hurry. The more important the problem, the more time we ask of ourselves or others for decision making. What parents would choose a school for their child in five minutes? Even when the task itself doesn't take very long, the first and most essential constituent of any decision-making process is time.

THE TOOLS: HEAD AND HEART

We usually don't pick up the telephone book, open to the Yellow Pages and, with our eyes closed, put our finger on any random entry in order to select the street where we'll live, the company where we'll work, or the school where we will send our child. We certainly do not want chance to make those decisions for us. As mature human beings we prefer to trust in better tools than luck for reaching a decision.

First, we use our head. We reflect on the situation, we look for information, we weigh the advantages and the disadvantages of our options, and we try to foresee the consequences of them. Sometimes we consult people whom we see as experts about schools, a certain job, or the area of the town under consideration. We collect and file away data on the problem we want to solve. After analyzing and synthesizing, we come to see, more objectively, a way to proceed. The word *objectively* implies that, at the end of our considerations, the solution that we have identified as possible, based on our data, would seem to be a reasonable choice to many other people as well.

But our head is rarely, if ever, the only part of ourselves involved in choices. All along, we consult our heart in order to verify whether or not the possible solution appeals to us. Objectively, this kind of house may respond to our needs, but we cannot picture ourselves living in such a wealthy and isolated area. This job may bring a good salary and provide the opportunity for an interesting promotion, but the idea of a future with so much time spent away from our family disturbs us. This school is renowned for its academic successes, but we, parents as well as child, do not feel at home in its snobbish atmosphere. In a word, our heart has something to say in our investigation, and we all know that the word said by our heart is often the last word when it comes to decision making.

So, we screen with our heart what we discover with our head in order to make a decision that is *ours* and one we can confirm subjectively. It's our decision. This means that others may understand our choice intellectually, without agreeing, because they may not value the same things we cherish. They may even judge us unreasonable.

The decision is really ours and ours alone. This is so true that it is possible to be aware of one's aloneness even with close friends. I may, for instance, discuss my problem with some friends I consider wise: "You know me well; tell me where you can picture me living, in the city or in a suburb? You have been with me for a long time; can you see me as a plumber or as a mail carrier? You have followed our child's life for years; what school would you recommend?" But, in the end, I know that the wise friend cannot decide for me. I am the one who has to move and shall live for years in a new environment. I am the one who shall carry the burden or savor the joy of a new job for quite a while. It is our child who shall undergo and deal with the results of the education that will mold her. The actual choice is, and remains, my choice. And sometimes, it is so much mine that I finally decide to act contrary to all of the advice that has been offered.

And this makes us recall that no responsible choice exists without inner freedom. No one else can make my decisions, neither my closest friends nor the most skilled experts. Of course, I may seek the aid of both friends and experts, but I must not let their opinions influence me to such an extent that I lose my internal freedom. This is fairly obvious, but what may not be so obvious is the need to stay free as well from any *subconscious motivations* that may direct my actions without my awareness or consent. In the opening sections of this book I describe the basic elements involved in the process of making a decision. In later chapters I will come back to the fundamental notion of inner freedom that is called into question each time that I use my head and my heart to choose.

THE CORNERSTONE: VALUES

The components that structure the decision-making process are already present when we select from a menu in a restaurant: time, intellect, and our emotions, which we call affectivity. But we are still missing one ingredient.

When life asks me to make choices, I usually weigh my options with respect to what is important to me. What leads me to consider cholesterol in my food selection is the value that I see, both intellectually and emotionally, in maintaining my health; this is important to me. It is the value I perceive in being in the city or in a suburb, in spending or investing a large amount of money, in having a certain kind of family life that directs me when I choose the place where I will live. It's the value I place on creativity, on a better salary, or on the social status that leads me to take a new job. It's the value I see in the qualities of the studies, of the environment, and the cultural fulfillment, of the human-being-to-come in our child that will push me to give priority to one school rather than another. I keep one goal before me, in my mind and in my heart, throughout the process that prepares me for and ends in my decision: to make my decision in the light of one or several values. Others may agree with me or not according to whether or not they understand and share my value system.

What has been said about the various components involved in the preparation of a decision can be summarized in one sentence: Influenced by our values, we work with our intellect and our affectivity in order to determine, in time, our decision.

The diagrams in Appendix 5 provide for an easy recall of the principal concepts.

———•———

So, there's nothing here that is mysterious or magical. We have simply described the typical structure of any human decision made seriously. Let us call such a process *discernment*.

It is time to go back to what we put aside earlier, the religious implications of a choice for someone who has a religious belief. For believers, the notion of discernment also implies God. So, from now on in this book, discernment will mean a systematic process of working in time with our intellect and affectivity, according to a value system illumined by faith. Thus, this book is a religious book, but, as I said in the Introduction, those who profess no religious belief will find, later in these pages, a translation of the method in secular terms.

So, what happens when, through religious belief, faith, we introduce God into the process that we have analyzed? First of all, faith does not change the structure we have just depicted. It would be a strange thing if we had to ignore, deny, or reject the framework or the tools that arise from the essence of our human condition in order to make a decision suitable to our

faith in God. They are gifts of our Creator. Even people of deep
faith have always to work in time and with their intellect and
affectivity when they want to discover what they call God's will
in their lives. The most inspired persons have been touched in
time, appealed to in their intellect and affectivity at the moment of their decisions. It cannot be otherwise, because we
cannot be other than human beings. We are living in time and
perceiving everything with our head and through our heart.
This is extremely significant, for it implies that as soon as, and
as long as, believers or nonbelievers use their heads and their
hearts, in time, for making decisions, they are faithful to God's
desire. And, if they do it well, God is content.

———◆———

FAITH AND VALUES

What gift, then, does religious belief bring to discernment? Faith brings with itself a set of values that are not always self-evident for a nonbeliever. Every religious revelation
speaks of God in a way that is shaped by the recipients' environment and culture. Therefore, revelation expresses the divine vocation of human beings according to their own traditions. In this way some values are determined for believers in
a particular tradition, values they accept, if they want to be
faithful to their God.

Believing Jews, for instance, try to remember that the cosmos is put into our hands, and that it depends on us to make it
succeed in spite of what makes it a "broken world" (as a French
philosopher said). Faithful Moslems, knowing that one of the
five pillars of their faith is almsgiving, try to practice that principle in their daily lives. Committed Christians try to keep in
mind that serving the lowliest one is a priority that cannot be
disputed or forgotten. (Mt 25: 31–46)

Of course, nonbelievers may prize participation in the cre-
ation of the cosmos, may cherish charity as a governing principle, and may value selfless service to the oppressed, and many

do so. But for Jews, Moslems, or Christians, such values have the weight of being connected with God's revelation itself.

This is so important that rejection of those values for these believers is sometimes greater than a mistake or a fault. It is a sin that affects their relationship with God and, at the extreme, their eternal life. Therefore, faith does not change the structure of discernment but gives it an additional meaning. As Teilhard de Chardin would say, what is at stake for a believer is no longer a simple human history, but God's design: "It is a question, in a true sense, of achieving the victory of no less than a God" *(The Divine Milieu).* * Being a part of God's plan also adds another dimension to their responsibility.

And, because of that, the faithful, whose actions are consistent with their beliefs, feel impelled to deepen their relationship with their God. They try to know more and more the divine message and its set of values. This may be done by studying the sacred texts, the traditions, theologies, customs, the life and writings of authentic witnesses—and by praying. Such involvement influences and imbues the work of the believer's intellect and affectivity.

FAITH AND INTELLECT

If we are believers, it does not mean that our intellect abdicates its responsibility or ignores its capacity for analyzing and judging because of the revelation we accept. Rather, our intellect is enlightened by the divine teaching. It is impossible to conceive of a contradiction between the human intellect and God's revelation, for God is the one who gives us both. On the contrary, we believe that God's work within us helps us to think more accurately because God's words rescue our intellect from many narrow traps: the pride of reason, for example, that claims to master the truth of everything, and the lies of ratio-

---

*Teilhard de Chardin, *The Divine Milieu* (New York: Harper and Row, 1960), 38.

nalization that repress the messages of the feelings. Faith denounces the vanity of money and power in themselves and shows us how to manage them for the service of the poor, for instance. Thus, faith purifies and enriches what immediately appears attractive and valuable to our intellect. "Do not conform yourselves to this age but be transformed by the renewal of your mind, so that you may judge what is God's will, what is good, pleasing and perfect," says Paul. (Rom 12: 2) The same help is offered to our affectivity.

FAITH AND AFFECTIVITY

Just as it was for our intellect, our affectivity does not have to abdicate when faith enters into a decision-making process. If God has given us a heart, it is not in order to ask us to put it aside in some circumstances. How would Christians be able to love if they did that? But the Christian revelation teaches our affectivity what love is really all about. We need to learn that love is not romance. It is service. This does not repudiate the ways in which nonbelievers love, but it makes those of us who are Christians aware of another dimension of love. We believe that it is God's life itself within us. When we love according to our Christian faith, "we make God exist" as Maurice Clavel, a French philosopher, said, because we make love present in this world through our own human flesh.

Faith also purifies our affectivity. It helps us to discover more and more clearly the traps, the disguises, and the deceits of our selfishness. Like the kind of snare furnished by a false sense of dedication when we are too good or too nice, or we choose to be peacemakers *at any price,* for example. Nonbelievers may make the same discoveries in other ways, but we Christians believe in the power of faith in these matters because, for us, God is Love, Love itself, and therefore an expert in the field. (1 Jn 4: 8) We can allow this expert to enlighten the depths of our being without fear because Love is full of compassion and mercy. We have only to give God's Spirit the greatest possible freedom within us. The purpose of this book is to increase that possibility.

This discernment is a process leading to a decision that uses the intellect and the affectivity, influenced by values that are enlightened and purified by faith, in a systematic way and without disregarding time.

Now, I must explain more concretely how we can accomplish all of this. I am going to describe the whole process step by step: the road between the question we have to answer and the result; the journey and its conclusion in a decision. But we need to know our ultimate destination.

CHAPTER

2

Discernment Is to Choose Methodically with God

Where can we find a concise expression of our ultimate destination? Since making decisions is an action as old as humankind, it is not surprising to see the question of discerning appearing in the first pages of the Bible. Adam and Eve had to discern…, but it is the author of the Book of Deuteronomy who gives Israel a kind of systematic principle in order to help God's People to stop making mistakes and to make better choices than before. The past had proven to the writer the dire consequences of wrong decisions.

Our Ultimate Destination: Life

In Deuteronomy 30: 15–20, we find the concise expression we need. God asserts that we face life and death: "Here, then, I have set before you life and prosperity, death and doom …. I have today set before you life and death, the blessing and the curse." And the Lord adds, "You, choose life."

We have there a simple principle that echoes many of our own experiences. Our decisions have led us sometimes to life, sometimes to death. For example:

—— Years ago, I chose my current job. I know that I did not correctly measure my strength. Today I am exhausted, physically and emotionally. The stress and the distance from my family life are destroying me.

—— The center of the city has been transformed into a commercial district where there are only offices. After office hours the place is empty and dead, dangerous when it gets dark. Why am I still living here?

—— After an initial period of adjustment, our child is very happy with her studies. Her imagination, her taste for discovery, her creativity are being fed and really blossoming.

—— We now live outside the city. Silence and nature give us rest and calm. We awake each morning feeling very alive.

—— He went as a volunteer to a developing country. The aloneness, the climate, the food, the fact of being a foreigner became less and less bearable. He developed a stomach ulcer and now he is depressed.

So, the Book of Deuteronomy is right: we choose life or death every time we make an important decision. Better, indeed, to choose life!

A METHOD IS WORTHWHILE

Why could the writer of Deuteronomy express so clearly and so specifically a basic principle of choosing? Probably because he wrote centuries after Moses and he had seen the bad fruit of the Jews' choices made before his time. "Any sound tree bears good fruit, while a decayed tree bears bad fruit." (Mt 7: 17)

But can we avoid waiting until the harvest, because by then it may be too late? Is it possible to have a systematic method of choosing what will guarantee good fruit? It is impossible beforehand to assure with absolute accuracy that what we are going to plant today will result in our own well-being and the well-being of others. If we retain the image of the fruit, we cannot forecast perfectly what tomorrow's weather will bring or the effect it will have on our seedlings. Will there be tornadoes or a gentle rain, drought or perfect sunshine? Who can predict? However, if a farmer methodically takes good care of the soil, prunes the fruit trees at the right time, uses the proper fertilizers and insecticides, and takes precautions against frost, good fruit may usually be anticipated. So also, a method of decision making reduces the hazards of being mistaken and puts the odds in our favor. "Choose Life" becomes, through a method, "Prepare the way of Life."

If we work with a systematic method of discernment, we abandon a kind of magical behavior that puts too much trust in what is sometimes called instinct or spontaneity, sometimes even inspiration (we'll see later that intuition is different). We reproach our children for a spontaneity that many times creates problems and even accidents; strangely enough, we frequently act impulsively and with little thought. It is as if we say to ourselves, "Don't look before you leap!" sure that our instinct or our inspiration comes directly from God. Most of the time this behavior results from being led by our most superficial emotions, the value and accuracy of which are at best questionable. We forget that inspiration for people such as scientists and inventors, musicians and artists, is the fruit of a long period of systematic searching, reflecting, and pondering.

But what about those we call mystics? Aren't they the symbols of a sudden and powerful inspiration? After all, what about Saul on the road to Damascus? Indeed, the first bloom of Saul's revelation reached him rather abruptly. But it took a long while for the fruit to appear: it was three long years of methodical gestation in the womb of God and the Church before Paul was delivered as the man we know now. (Ga 1: 11–24) All ripe fruit, when it is finally harvested and delivered, has undergone a maturation often accomplished by methodical labor.

Unfortunately, events frequently do not give us much time for planning. Will a method do any good in these circumstances? When a fire breaks out in a motel where we are staying, we do whatever we can and as quickly as possible to escape. However, there too, a method is very helpful. If we have, beforehand and methodically, read and analyzed the map of the building, which is usually posted on the door, we will be able to find our escape route quickly. Soldiers are trained systematically before being sent to the front line in order to acquire the right *reflexes* for sudden emergencies when they are under fire. (There, once more, it is impossible to guarantee that the training will always work for each soldier. Without training, however, his behavior would be problematic.) Thus, a method will give us, over time, reflexes for choosing life and not death.

The advantage of a method in developing discernment becomes evident with some reflection. The planes or cars that will be sold on the market in ten more years are already being planned, methodically, in research departments. The lives of astronauts depend on months of preflight systematic calculations and tests by scientists and engineers. We only fully make any food recipe our own after several methodical trials. And yet, we are willing to risk our lives by making decisions instinctively, without the benefit of a method! Decision making is not like making instant coffee; there is much more at stake — life and death — as Deuteronomy says.

At this point in our journey, we have identified, in a general way, all the ingredients for discernment: time is the framework, intellect and affectivity are the tools, values enlightened by faith are the cornerstone. And Deuteronomy has contributed the final principle: choose Life instead of Death. We now understand that it is safer and more effective to learn and practice a method than to act impulsively.

In the following chapters I describe how we can work methodically with our intellect and our affectivity under the influence of our values enlightened by our Christian faith, in order to choose Life and not Death in our decisions.

Let me make clear that what I am going to develop concerns exclusively the discernment made by *an individual person* in order to come to his or her personal decisions. In some later chapters I will propose an application of the same method to the case of a group that wishes to make a common decision.

QUESTIONS

It may be helpful, at this point, to summarize the elements of discernment we have explored by questions that readers may ask themselves. So far, we have talked about time, intellect (head),* affectivity (heart),* values, faith, a principle, and a method.

TIME

In the past:

—— In which decisions did I undergo needless anxieties and worries just because I postponed my decision too long?

—— Which decisions did not bear good fruit because I made them too quickly?

—— How much pressure did I put on myself in order to get an "instant product"?

In the present:

—— Taking into account the degree of importance of a decision to come, how much time will I allow myself to make it?

—— If I have the tendency to postpone a decision (in fact to let other people or events decide for me), how will I prevent this inclination from getting the upper hand?

—— What is my own pace of processing anything; is it usually fast or slow? How will I modify this?

HEAD

In the past:

—— When I made up my mind impulsively, what were the results? What was missing in terms of intellectual reasoning?

In the present:

—— If I am facing a decision to be made, what will my intellectual method be?

---

* Do I take into account the two sides of my brain? (See Roger H. Sperry, Nobel Laureate in Medicine, 1981). If I am intellectually oriented, what do I do to listen to my feelings; if I am a "feeling person" by nature, how do I balance this with reasoning?

HEART

In the past:

—— What happened when I made decisions without consulting my heart? How did I feel afterwards, in the short run? in the long run?

In the present:

—— If I am making a decision now, how am I taking into account my "gut reactions"?

VALUES

In the past:

—— What are my most cherished values? How did I respect their hierarchy in my most recent decisions?

In the present:

—— What values are implied in the choice I am facing right now? How do they match with mine? How will I safeguard my values by my choice?

FAITH

In the past:

—— How was my faith involved in my recent decisions? How did I pray while discerning?

In the present:

—— How am I going to consult God for my coming decisions?

PRINCIPLE

In the past:

—— Which of my decisions have been life-giving? Which decisions have led to "death"?

In the present:

—— Why do some of the decisions I am facing now seem, for me, "enlivening" or "stifling"?

METHOD

In the past:

—— How much have my past decisions resembled a poker game?

—— Which of my spontaneous "inspirations" have been really fruitful in the long run?

In the present:

—— What method will I use to "take charge" of my future decisions?

PART TWO

Discernment by an Individual Person

CHAPTER

1

How to Work with My Head

In Deuteronomy 30, God enjoins Israel to keep "his commandments, statutes and decrees." Deuteronomy, as a whole, is a discourse aimed at informing the intellect of the reader in several ways. First, by a new interpretation of the history of Israel, God's People, enriched by the experience of her faults. Then, by a new wording of the Charter of the Covenant, the Ten Commandments (Dt 5). And finally, through the Deuteronomic Code. This is the Law whose core is the Decalogue that promotes the values with which we are all familiar. The writer further elaborates the content of this law by proposing many other values that involve clean and unclean animals, Hebrew slaves, marriage, and other aspects of life. The Law must be known in order to be practiced. Following this example, let us recall the core of the Christian faith that our intellect is called to know and apply to any discernment in order to make a decision that leads to life.

OUR CHRISTIAN VOCATION: AGAPE

As Christians we believe that God saved us through Christ and gave us the Spirit. Made God's sons and daughters we live God's life itself by the Spirit: Love, *Agape*. Agape is the Greek word used by the writers of the New Testament when they talk about love. Agape means loving, but loving as doing and working for the good and growth of others. We see that the real Christian notion of love has little to do with the current image of love portrayed by the media. It may or may not include a warm feeling of empathy, for, above all, it is serving. Loving does not necessarily imply liking. That is why Jesus could say, "Love your enemy." It is always possible to serve someone else, even the one we do not like. (Mt 5: 43–48) Jesus summarized the Law and the Prophets in a new commandment directing us to love our neighbor as he did. Taught by our faith, we know intellectually therefore that we are invited to choose Life, include Agape in all our decisions. (Ph 1: 9–10) We must imitate Jesus, do as he did, as Paul says, because he was, he still is for us the authentic human being permitting the Spirit of Agape complete freedom in himself. (Ph 2: 5)

Jesus, Perfect Agape in Human Flesh

The behavior of Jesus that demonstrates a loving attitude and teaches us what acting with love really means is reflected in many texts: for instance, in the chant of the Beatitudes and the early Christian hymn recorded by Paul in Philippians. (Mt 5: 2–12; Ph 2: 5–11) For our purpose let's examine another "song," proclaimed by an adversary, Caiphas. According to John's own words, it resounds with the truth.

John writes, "It was as High Priest that he made this prophecy that Jesus was to die for the nation — and not for the nation only, but to gather together in unity the scattered children of God." (11: 51)

It's this representation of Jesus that we will analyze, listening to the four melodies always present in the life of Christ, melodies characteristic of a human life perfectly led by the Spirit of Agape. Why the word *melody*? Because only a poetic image can do justice to love. The love that we are talking about defies all definitions. The four melodies that I will mention suggest the four parts that are sung in a piece written for several voices: soprano, alto, tenor, and bass, like the *Messiah* by Handel. Who has not enjoyed the Hallelujah Chorus at Christmas?

THE FOUR MELODIES OF AGAPE

Jesus is the Melody of Incarnation.

For those of us who are Christian, the word *Jesus* is the personal name of God's Son who was a specific human being, a man from a particular place, Nazareth in Palestine. He lived within a given tradition and time, and died in Jerusalem around the year 33. In that single word we sum up the Christian revelation: God's Word was made flesh through the *Incarnation.* (Jn 1: 14; Ph 2: 6–7)

The Word of God emptying himself, knew and accepted our human condition in all things — but sin, says Christian faith. (Ph 2: 7) The texts of the Gospels describe Jesus as a Jewish baby and as an ordinary man. We see him eating and drinking, crying or rejoicing, feeling tired or angry, tempted, distressed by fear, suffering and dying. He speaks the Aramaic language and follows the customs of his society and his religion. He is a real human being grounded in all the obligations, the limitations and the fulfillment of our physical, social, and spiritual reality, according to his time, culture, and tradition.

The first melody that can be heard in the life of Jesus, then, is *Incarnation.* Many texts in the Gospels focus on incarnation and give us a picture of the man of Nazareth living God's life.

The Requiem of Jesus is that he "was to die."

We Christians assert that Jesus, God-Agape made one of us, spent his life loving in two ways: *giving and being given up* to people until death.

Giving implies the initiative and the control of the giver. Jesus is continually giving till the end. He gives his teaching and attention, his presence and time. He feeds people even to the point of the gift of his body and blood through bread and wine. Eventually he gives his life. (Jn 13: 1)

Although being given up can also be initiated by the one giving himself or herself up, the control of the action belongs to the one who receives the gift. Jesus is given up, handed over to others as a baby, as a public person, as a convicted, tortured, and executed criminal. "Into your hands, Father, I commit my spirit" sums up his gift and abandonment. The ultimate of Agape includes the abandonment of self into the other's hands.

The Anthem of universality is in his death "... not for the nation only but ... [for] the ... children of God."

Clearly, this assertion of John expands the salvation accomplished in the life and death of Jesus to all peoples, far beyond the usual Jewish notion of God's chosen People. Christ is the Savior of humankind in its *universality*. To be sure, this was already rooted in Abraham's blessing, but it was manifested in the experience of the early Church and summed up by Paul when he wrote, "... and there are no more distinctions between Jew and Greek, slave and free, male and female." (Ga 3: 28)

If we look for manifestations of this quality in the life of Jesus, we notice that he never rejects anyone. He welcomes heretics and public sinners, like the Samaritans or Zacchaeus. He is available for Pagans or for Pharisees like the Canaanite woman and the Roman centurion, like Simon and Nicodemus. He welcomes lepers, the rich and the poor, women and children. He is there for officials or outcasts like Jairus or people who are possessed. And, among the Twelve, he accepts Matthew and Simon, even though the tax collector had worked for the Romans and the Zealot had fought against them.

A hymn of communion, for he died "... to gather together the scattered children of God."

The mission of Jesus aimed at reconciliation: the *communion* of all with God and with one another. As Paul says, "... all of you are one in Christ Jesus." (Ga 3: 28)

It is true that his message and deeds divide the Jews, as we can see, for instance, in John 7: 11–13, 40–44, but he is obviously seeking a communion among people. Most of his miracles reintegrate the person that he cures into society. And his teaching very often emphasizes the perfect tool for reconciliation and communion, forgiveness. He expresses his desire earnestly when he says, "Jerusalem, Jerusalem … how often have I longed to gather your children, as a hen gathers her chicks under her wings, and you refused!" (Mt 23: 37) That wish will be realized in the early Church to a greater extent than he seems able to see when he responds to the Canaanite woman. (Acts; Mt 15: 24)

THE FOUR CRITERIA OF DISCERNMENT

Thus, our intellect enlightened by faith understands through the behavior of Jesus what a human life impregnated by the Spirit of Agape is like. This Life is the one we are called to choose in our decisions. And because we believe that the same Spirit of Jesus dwells within us, we can recognize with our intellect the choices that give us a greater possibility of living according to this Spirit of loving. (1 Co 3: 16) We can use the *four criteria* that we extract from what we have discovered through the Gospels to analyze the different alternatives we are facing.

Our intellect has the task of finding the solution in which we will have more of a chance to be *incarnate, giving and given up, universal, and in communion.*

One way to use the four criteria in our discernment process is to ask ourselves certain questions whenever we are confronted with a choice.* Our questions may be expressed in words like these:

Which solution will give me the opportunity to be incarnate:

—— to be the one I am, and no one else;

---

* The Appendix entitled *More about the Four Criteria,* gives a more developed list of possible questions.

—— to accept other people as they are, not as I would like them to be;

—— to accept the facts as I discover them to be, through a serious and objective analysis;

—— to accept the "here and now" of the situation I am dealing with?

Which solution will give me the possibility of giving and being given up:

—— to give what I have and who I am;

—— to be given up through openness, welcoming, and vulnerability?

Which solution will open my person to universality, in space and time, to the point that I dare:

—— to be open to all the areas of my being and of my life;

—— to be open to all the currents of the society I live in, past, present, and coming;

—— to be open to all the people around me?

Which solution will best permit me:

—— to be reconciled and in harmony with myself;

—— to be a part of the different wholes I belong to;

—— to weave bonds among the ones I meet, to build communion among and with them;

—— to act against all discrimination and for reconciliation while respecting the differences among people?

So, when two alternatives are placed before me, my intellect will choose Life through the solution that best meets the four criteria and thus offers the greatest possibility to follow the Spirit, to live Agape.

PERFECTIONISM, HEROISM OR CHRISTIAN REALISM?

We believe that Jesus Christ was the perfect YES to Agape and the only One forever. (2 Co 1: 18) But what about ourselves? Is the process of discernment that we have described merely a Christian *ideal* impossible to reach? No, for then we would be saying that God is playing games with us through Christ. We believe that God's Spirit is working within us with respect for our humanity, for the limitations of the human beings we are, and for our need to keep growing until we die. We look at our life as a history, never perfectly accomplished, always *unfinished*, but always penetrated by the dynamism and power of Agape. This is our daily experience: we are the dough unceasingly raised up by the yeast of Love. (Mt 13: 33)

This conviction removes the unhealthy tendency toward perfectionism and allows us to work realistically with our intellect when we try to discern. Rather than ask ourselves which solution will give us the possibility to be incarnate, giving and given up, universal, and in communion, let's probe ourselves with a humbler question that will deliberately include the idea of growth. The wording of the wiser question might be this:

Which solution will give me an opportunity to take *one more step ahead* toward being incarnate, giving and given up, universal, and in communion?

Taking one more step ahead: this correction of the text already provides a way out of two temptations. First, it prevents us from refusing Agape in our lives with the excuse, "I cannot fly so high," and putting the responsibility of Love in the world on others' shoulders — as we might do when we see the works of extraordinary witnesses. Second, it militates against our subtle and proud attraction for spectacular exploits and heroic virtues, for we are not called for Olympic spiritual games. If taking one step at a time seems rather commonplace, let us remember that the Son of God spent nine-tenths of his life as a common ordinary man, a carpenter in Nazareth, and that the Gospel points out that he also grew. (Lk 2: 40, 52)

This slight correction may seem like nothing, but it allows us to take ourselves where we are, and not where we would like to be, and cannot be. If we really cannot take longer strides, God certainly does not ask the impossible. "Here is my servant who I have chosen ... He will not break the crushed reed, nor put out the smoldering wick," said the Lord through Jesus and Isaiah. (Mt 12: 20; Is 42: 3) Yes, our correction implies growth, but a growth that is really possible for everyone. Therefore, it acknowledges the capacity of each one to answer God's call for Agape. It reveals, for instance, that socially or psychologically handicapped persons, taken where they are in their own situation, can love. A prostitute (or a tax collector, Mt 21: 31) and a retarded child can always make one more step ahead in Love, starting from where they are, and not from where they should be according to some official, formal, or usual standards. For people who are emotionally disturbed or mentally ill, that one more step may even remain in the more or less conscious intention, known by God alone. Even its external manifestation may be relatively invisible or not in accordance with our accustomed secular or religious norms. The Lord "does not judge by appearances." (Is 11: 3) If we are inclined to judge or condemn anyone's conscience, remembering the one more step ahead will remove this temptation.

Finally, one more step sends us back to live Agape in any action, even the smallest. Jesus himself said, "If you can trust someone in little things you can also trust that person in greater." (Lk 16: 10) In this case he was talking about money, but his comment can be applied to everything. His words allow us to hope that, if events demand our heroism someday, our fidelity to Agape in the little things of every day will give us the necessary strength for loving until the end.

Similarly, what we have just said about people can also be applied to situations, circumstances, or environments. At first glance, many might deny the possibility of seeing Love present during a strike, in the midst of a war, or in a prison because of the conflicts and violences that fill those events or places. Yet, that would be a false assumption: if Christ went down to Hell, as we believe he did, he can be anywhere by his Spirit — as a German theologian wrote years ago. No situation, no place is so harsh that it is impossible to start, to take one more step in Love. Not one of us — striker, soldier, prisoner, correctional officer, politician, diplomat, person in business—is ever in a place or in circumstances where harmony reigns. Nonetheless, though it may be a challenge to our creativity, it is always possible to invent one more step toward Life and Love. And if we permit the Spirit of Love free reign, harmonizing with the melodies of Agape, it is conceivable that we might even transform a halting step into a dance. (Zp 3: 17)

A FIFTH CRITERION

In this way then, when we are faced with a number of alternatives we can work with our intellect and, helped by our faith, determine the way of Life, the way of Agape. Why is it then that history is full of the mistakes made by Christians? Jesus warned his own, "Be on guard! Let no one mislead you. Many will come attempting to impersonate me. 'I am the Messiah!' they will claim, and they will deceive many." (Mt 24: 4-5) The warning has not always been heeded, and Christians and other people, deceiving themselves or deluded by others, have chosen the path of Death. What was missing in their discernment?

Let us take the case of a European country some years ago where there were some people who were extremely incarnate — very aware of their common heritage, culture, and values. They were giving a great deal and willing to be given up right to the point that many died for their nation. No doubt they experienced an intense communion among themselves — their motto was, "One People, One Culture, One Leader" ("Ein Volk, Ein Kultur, Ein Führer"). The fact is that there were many Christians, among others, who were caught in their trap. The readers who have recognized them realize that we have been describing the Nazis, in Germany, between 1930 and 1945. What was missed in Christians' discernment that so many were deceived by Hitler?

Counterfeits of Christian behavior can result when *one of the four melodies is missing.* The Nazis, for example, were not universal: they wanted to eliminate some political, ethnic, and religious groups such as Communists, Gypsies, and Jews; they wanted to conquer the world and submit everybody to their dictatorship. They lacked the criterion of universality. Therefore, when we analyze our alternatives before making a decision, we must keep all four criteria together in our mind. If, in one of our potential solutions, one of the four criteria is missing, the chances are that it is a counterfeit solution and that it will not eventually lead us to Life. So, here we have a fifth criterion of discernment: Agape cannot be divided up into slices, and one of which ignored. We need *to use the four criteria as a whole.* To be sure, an emphasis might be placed on one of the melodies, depending on the time, the place, or the circumstances, but all four must be there like the four-part harmony of a Bach chorale. No element can be missing. Using another image, we could compare this kind of integrity or wholeness with the distinct liturgical seasons: each season highlights a particular melody, but all the parts of the symphony encompassing *all* of Agape must be played.

Confirming, for Christians, this test of the spirits, Paul has already told us that "speaking with human tongues and angelic as well ... having the gift of prophecy and with full knowledge ... having faith great enough to move mountains ... giving everything to feed the poor ... giving our body to be burned" are never a guarantee of authenticity. (1 Co 13) We can only trust Agape.

But It Is Necessary to Complete the Work of Our Intellect

I want to summarize here and pull together what I have said so far about the work of the intellect in the discernment process.

- When we reach any decision point in our lives, it is as if we have come to a crossroads. We must make a choice and select the way leading to Life, to Agape for those of us who are Christian.

- After we have determined our alternatives, we remind ourselves, globally, of our Christian vocation, the general direction of our journey (others must remind themselves of the values of their own tradition). We do this because the specific road we are going to take, here and now, must be oriented in that direction. Otherwise the whole trip is compromised before we even start.
- Then, working with our intellect, we screen the possible solutions, using the four criteria given by our values enlightened and purified by our faith. We carefully examine each road in the light of each one of them, overlooking none. Our objective is to find the road that will allow us to go toward Agape (or the realization of our values). Knowing that no road is perfect, our car may break down, and unforeseen things over which we have no control may occur along the way, we do all we can to discern.
- Once we have found the way, we make up our mind, and go.

Here is a good example of the use of the intellect in decision making. Andrew, one of my students, a senior in high school, explained to me how he had come to choose a particular profession:

—— Led by a desire to expand his horizons and to be useful, he wanted to go and work in developing Africa.

—— Exposure to reading and television, as well as lectures in school, had made him very aware of Third-World conditions. He knew, for instance, that global literacy was still unachieved, that health services were inaccessible to the majority of the rural people, and that lack of adequate infrastructure for transportation slowed the pace at which the country could develop itself.

—— He came to the conclusion that some possible ways of working in Africa might be through teaching, medicine, or public works.

—— Knowing well the one he was, he was quickly able to eliminate teaching: he had no skill with children. Analyzing his abilities with regard to public works and medicine, he real-

ized that engineering made better use of his particular intellectual powers (he loved math, he had a knack for problem solving in physics, and he hated blood and gut).
—— So, he enrolled in a university program leading to a civil
engineering degree. His specialty would be roads and
bridges.

Eventually he went to Africa and, while creating many
roads he shared his expertise with local engineers. His bridge-
building was a very concrete way to establish communion. It is
not difficult to recognize that Andrew, in his own way, was attuned to the four melodies of Agape that I have described.

Using the intellect is only a part of the whole process of
discernment. We have to complete the work done by the intellect with the help of our affectivity. It might be dangerous
not to do so.

Let us suppose that, at the end of the process I have just
shown, I come to the conclusion in my mind that "it is this solution and not the other one that will lead me to Life." It seems
that I have really answered the question, "What is possible here
and now?" Have I, in fact, reached the objective conclusion, the
truth? To the degree that I have effectively worked with my intellect, I might presume that many people who accept the same
religious message or values that I do would agree with my
choice. In fact, what I have come up with is not as objective as
it might appear; it is not the truth. The work of my intellect
gives me a somewhat objective solution, but only partially objective, for the work has been done by my own mind, and I can
never claim to be able to encompass the truth.

Perhaps it is better that a perfectly objective analysis is not
possible for any individual person or any group. If it were possible, certain people would be tempted to establish, once and
for all, the answers to all the questions (using computers, for
example.) They, then, might claim that they had the ability to
express the Truth. Such absolutism could lead to despotism. Of
course, it is always helpful to listen to experts in any field, but

how difficult it is to remain free when every day we are invited to accept the messages of the media, the trendsetters, the leaders of different institutions, etc.? All of them claim they know what you and I must do!

Such claims play on a sensitive part in each of us where an easy credulity is always ready to operate. We are tempted to believe that, somewhere, someone has what we don't have, knows what we don't know, knows on our behalf. That is why we are ready to abdicate our responsibility and to submit ourselves to gurus we believe to be inspired. But "who knows a man's [or woman's] innermost self but the man's spirit within him." (1 Co 2: 11–12) The claim to knowledge by any authority, in the name of old traditions or new sciences, does not change the fact that our being has its word to say. This does not destroy regard for legitimate authority and expertise or devalue our own objective conclusion. It merely emphasizes the necessity of listening to our heart that feels and knows in its own way.

As a matter of fact, our reasoning is never purely intellectual. Our fascination with sciences leads us to accept the myth of rationality too easily. A good example is the belief that emotions are out of place in the business world. But everyone knows how many business people suffer from stress, heart attacks, guilt, and nervous breakdowns. A simple stomach ulcer can illustrate the fact that our intellect is never totally disconnected from our affectivity. Our mind can never get rid of our heart, of our guts. Therefore, the process is never finished for me as long as I have not presented the conclusions of my intellect to my affectivity in order to hear the answer to the real and definitive question, "What is possible, here and now, *for me*?"

Teaching Israel how to discern the Lord's ways, the author of Deuteronomy does not forget to take the counsel of the heart. (30: 17) Belonging to the Jewish culture, expressing this in his language, he could never separate understanding and feeling, as we claim we can. Strictly speaking, the fruit of discernment is a personal certainty produced by my heart *and* my head. Verifying the analysis of my intellect by the response of my affectivity will allow me to see if the solution that resulted can be a solution *for me*, and so the object of *my own* decision.

A choice is a *preference* that includes the heart and freedom. A very simple example can illustrate what I mean. Suppose I wish to get married. Here is a woman whom my intellect points out as a good choice: she is around my age and in good health; she believes in the same values as I do; we share the same cultural background; we enjoy most of the same things, but, I do not love her! Faced with all the reasons of my mind, my heart says no. "The heart has reasons that reason does not know," said Pascal.

Jesus gives us several examples of this. For instance, at twelve, on the occasion of his religious maturity, he enters the Temple for the first time. Objectively he might have gone back to Nazareth, obeying his parents according to what was expected of a child of that age. He did not, for his heart told him that he had to be "about his Father's business." (Lk 2: 41–52) Later also, certainly after integrating the objective content of his traditions, he felt impelled to go to John the Baptist, at the Jordan River. There, he heard in his heart, "You are my beloved Son. On you my favor rests." (Mk 1: 11) After a period of discernment in the desert, he decided that, even though it had been good to be a carpenter, it was now time to announce his Good News.

The Lord speaks through our intellect, but also to our heart, and we can learn to listen to God at that level. (Hos 2: 14, 16)*

---

* It is within the Christian context of Agape that the four criteria have been established and explained. But I am convinced that people who are neither Christian nor believers can use this method. See the Appendix entitled *Is This Method Only for Christians?*

CHAPTER
2

*How to Listen
to My Heart*

WHAT IS AFFECTIVITY?

I have often used the word *affectivity* in this text, but, before explaining how we can work with that characteristic of our being, we need to consider the meaning of the word. The dictionary defines the concept as "the ability to feel emotions: the division of mental life and activity relating to the emotions." Our capacity to be "touched" or "shaken"— affected, by someone or by something. This intimate vulnerability is revealed to us through the slow and steady, or sudden and explosive rising within us of what we call affection, emotion, feeling, humor, mood, impression, sentiment, or passion. All these words are more or less synonymous and each one, according to Webster, "implies a contrast with judgment and connotes a lack of thought." Emotions are always moving like waves within us. When we have to deal with a certain situation, we may be excited or depressed by it; we may like it or we may hate it. Somewhere within ourselves we experience either pleasure or trouble, delight or distress, depending upon the impact of the events. We have very little control over what catches and surprises, touches and moves, rouses and stirs us; practically no control at all when we are possessed by the extreme of passion.

THREE LAYERS OF EMOTIONS

When we hear people talking about their emotions, it is easy to observe that all the feelings they describe do not take place at the same level of experience. We all recognize when we are momentarily or deeply aggravated or happy, for example. Since in the following chapters it will be important to be able to distinguish between the different levels of affectivity, we will present a picture here that is quite simplified, but adequate for our purpose. Let us say that it seems we all have three "layers" of affectivity that we may visualize as three concentric circles, like the crust, the mantle, and the core of the earth.

The first circle, the outer one, seems to be made up of the most immediate and fleeting emotions, our spontaneous reactions. At this level, the feelings appear and disappear quickly, changing rapidly, even though they may move us very strongly for the moment. We may leap from laughter to tears in a few minutes. Touched by someone or something, we may become thrilled with delight or gripped by anger on the spot. These feelings are like the choppy waves on the surface of the ocean that is never completely quiet. We will all acknowledge that these emotions are "superficial" because they do not express the deepest part of our personality. Sometimes, as a defense system, they may even hide what's really going on. I may look shy on the surface, but that may mask my stubbornness or even aggressivity. I may appear to be very outspoken, but I am full of fears at a deeper level.

It is evident that working with our affectivity in the process of discerning cannot take place within this layer; our immediate reactions are too quick and changeable. We have all known the poor quality of the information given us there: how many people or things have we liked or disliked "at first sight," and then time and experience proved that our first reaction was wrong. So, the point is not to let ourselves be led or trapped by our emotions when they occur at that level. If we do so, we will be like "flotsam and jetsam" at the mercy of continually changing currents. As far as we are able, and as soon as we can, we need to leave this outer layer and dive deep within ourselves. The depths of our ocean cannot be so easily disturbed by the winds that ruffle the surface.

We rarely feel the deepest level of our affectivity. Although we do not know everything about human nature, we will call it the center or the core of ourselves. At certain moments in our life, we get in touch with a feeling of clarity about who we are that has no equivalent in previous experiences. It is accompanied by an extremely deep happiness that sometimes dissolves space and time and is very difficult to put into words. At that specific moment we have a feeling of certainty that tells us "where" we are with no room for any doubt. We "know," but in a way that has little to do with intellectual reasoning: *a truth is there*; it is simply a *fact*. It is so powerful that the body may be shaken or totally impregnated by an inexpressible delight that may last quietly for days.

But it is important to know that this experience occurs rarely in life. When people say that they are often in touch with that level of being and certainty, we should be cautious about accepting their assertions at face value. When we look at the life of the most credible mystics of any religion, for instance, we see that such an experience is infrequent. Even psychotherapists agree that peak experiences in therapy are not the norm. It would be wonderful to become conscious at such a level each time we have to make a choice, for the feeling of clarity and certainty that we experience would be outstandingly helpful. But as we have said, such an experience is so rare in a lifetime that it would be better not to wait for it. If it comes, we can be grateful. If it does not, we need to use our tools in a more ordinary way. And even better to accept that we may never know our deepest selves. Only God can touch and reveal to us what we might call our "soul." But that special experience cannot be produced on demand.

Somewhere between the outer layer and the core is another stratum. We all have experiences that make us aware of its presence and, particularly, by contrast with the outer layer.

—— I have a severe headache: even though it is painful and irritating at a superficial level, deep within myself I feel at peace.
—— I have lost my Dad whom I loved very much: nearer the "surface" I feel sad and I may even cry. But, because his death has been the culmination of his life for him, descending to a deeper level of my being, I feel a kind of joy and thankfulness.
—— During a party, I am the clown of the group. I laugh and make people laugh. However, deep down, I cannot get rid of a feeling of sadness and disgust about the whole evening.

Sometimes it is not easy to perceive the line separating two levels, for it's never as distinct as a diagram. However, the above examples may send us back to the experiences we all have had that reveal two different levels of feeling. How can we characterize that middle level of affectivity? There, the emotions are not as numerous and changing as they are on the surface level, and they usually last fairly long. No matter what the events of daily life may bring, this is like a "home" where happiness or unhappiness can stay and deepen as long as there is nothing strong enough to change this. We sometimes see people caught in the grip of a "profound" sadness that they cannot get away from, just as we see others who are in a serenity that ordinary events cannot disturb. In the following chapters, when I talk about "emotion" or "feeling," I will be referring *exclusively* to this median layer. The reason is that the feelings experienced there reveal something more profound about ourselves than the superficial ones.

In order to work with our affectivity, we understand that we first need to be able to get in touch with the emotions present at this level, our "gut feelings," so that we can decode the messages they send us. This requires our being able to plunge to the depth where we hear the symphony or cacophony playing, or allow the expression to rise freely. For the feelings coming from that inside place can be compared to a music, carrying a message to our consciousness.

The awareness of this level requires a receptive silence. We cannot hear clearly someone whispering if the radio or the television is blaring, and we cannot hear the deepest levels of our affectivity if our life is full of noise. Static invading our inner attention, like external noise, prevents us from listening carefully to what is going on deep within ourselves. Putting aside the noise of our life, gently but firmly, through a kind of inner silence, is very helpful. Quietude and calm, solitude and silence, have to be learned and practiced, especially today when our environment is so full of the din of the unnecessary, the unessential. To decipher the message of our feelings let's go back to the Book of Deuteronomy.

LIFE, LOVE, AND DEATH

The Book of Deuteronomy invited us to choose Life and not Death. That choice lies within us. But let us describe Life, Love, and Death before explaining how to work with our heart.

We may choose to follow the surge of life rising up within us. It is God's gift. It is our impulse to be and to grow, to exult and be happy. It is our inclination to be curious and enthusiastic for discovery. It is our capacity for creating, inventing, and undertaking. It is our ability to start again and again, to persevere and to contend. (Ga 5: 22–23) We see this readily in a child's energy and dynamism before a challenge. And some capacity for this "life" remains with us always.

But for Christians, God-Life is also Agape, the source of the power of loving. We experience it with its tendency to go out to others, to accept, join, and to enjoy them. We feel it with its attraction for being one with other people, working and creating with them, serving them. We know it with its hunger for communion that leads to forgiveness, mercy, and reconciliation when it is necessary. Life and Love echo within us the presence of God's Spirit's "desire" and "groaning"—that One who "gives witness with our spirit that we are all children of God." (Rom 8: 16, 26–27)

However, as human beings we also harbor a grave vulnerability. "Through one man's disobedience [we] are all made sinners," and, since Adam and Eve, sin and death are our companions. (Rom 5: 12–19) "Powerless" people, we bear a permanent wound on which all our temptations play. (Rom 5: 6) When we succumb to these temptations, we open the way to death in all its forms, we bear "fruit for death." (Rom 7: 5) We are vulnerable to underrate and scorn, envy and covet, mock and crush, resent and detest, exploit and seek revenge, calumniate, torture, destroy, and even kill. We are open to damage or destruction by slavery to our addictions: our lust for money and career, reputation and power, our servitude to alcohol and drugs.

When we leave Life and Love for the paths of Death, the victims can be ourselves or other people. The law can be a guardrail, but guardrails can be broken.

It's at the very depth of our being that the choice of Life-Love or Death takes place and this choice will affect all of our decisions. Our choice makes us "mundane" or "spiritual." "Those who live according to the flesh are intent on the things of the flesh, those who live according to the spirit, on those of the spirit. The tendency of the flesh is toward death but that of the spirit toward life and peace." (Rom 8: 5–6)

We might conclude from all this that it is dangerous to hurt ourselves or others by following the lead of death. Thus we put ourselves among "the wicked who with hands and words invited death, considered it a friend, and pined for it, and made a covenant with it, because they deserve to be in its possession." (Wis 1: 16) It is better to choose and do what gives us the possibility of seeing Life-Love increase in our existence. Paul says, "If you live according to the flesh, you will die ..." (Rom 8: 13)

To be alive is usually our deepest desire. God's desire for us is the same. "Court not death by your erring way of life, nor draw to yourselves destruction by the works of your hands. Because God did not make death, nor does the Lord rejoice in the destruction of the living." For God "fashioned all things that they might have being," asserts the Book of Wisdom. (1: 13–14) For God is the One "who gives to all life and breath," in whom "we live and move and have our being," as Paul repeated with the same faith. (Acts 17: 25, 28)

Jesus, deepening and enlarging upon this tradition, while fighting with passion for Life and Love, said, "I have come that they might have life and have it to the full." (Jn 10: 10) This Life is Agape — the love of God, oneself, and neighbor, serving with the mercy demonstrated by the compassionate Samaritan and highly praised by Jesus when he replied to a lawyer, "Do this and you shall live." (Lk 10: 25–37)

THE METHOD

Now that we have described what we mean by Life-Love and Death, we may ask the question, "How do we work with our heart when we discern?" Suppose that I have before me the results of what I have been working on with my intellect. I have analyzed the alternatives and have determined "objectively" which of the possible solutions will lead me to Agape. Now I want to use my affectivity to verify whether or not this solution really suits *me*. I need to let my heart tell me if this is actually a solution for *me*. If so, it can become *my* decision, and a decision for Life and not Death *for and through* me. In order to understand how to go about this phase of discernment, we need to look at a rather common phenomenon.

Our being reacts to everything that happens to us. For example, if we perceive our experience as good, we savor pleasure. If we sense danger, on the other hand, we may be grasped by fear.

—— Offhandedly, my friend mentions my age. Immediately I perceive a threat and I feel displeasure, as if my friend had meant, "You are no longer very useful for us."

—— Someone wishes me a "Happy Birthday." I feel really good, as if the wisher assured me, "See, I am not ignoring you; I care about you."

—— A police officer stops me on the road. I panic. The child's anxiety in me says, "I got caught, I'll be punished!"

—— I have finally spotted a parking place and someone darts in just ahead of me. Anger flares in my "guts" and I feel like punching the intruder.

—— An elderly, blind man trying to cross the streets looks so lost and helpless that my heart melts: I can't help following my urge to guide the poor pedestrian.

These familiar examples have a simple underlying structure. Something happens and it touches something within me: *I get a feeling.* And such a feeling is connected with Life-Love and Death in me. If something occurs and touches the capacity for Life and Love within me, I get an *enlivening* feeling. In another situation, something occurs that touches the susceptibility for Death within me, and I get a *stifling* feeling.

—— My mother gives me the "silent treatment." I feel myself shrinking inside, even though I'm forty-five years old.

—— My neighbor greets me early in the morning and notices my new blouse. She makes my day, though I have the flu.

—— I am going to lose my job; I start sending résumés. Strangely enough, the challenge of the situation gives me an unusual energy.

Sometimes my feeling response may be entirely unexpected. What would console most people leaves me disconsolate; what other days I find troublesome today brings peace.

—— Stricken by a cancer, I am in excruciating pain. Before Jesus on the cross, I am invaded by a great relief.

—— At my little boy's funeral, the minister describes the beauty of Heaven; I get angrier and angrier.

The underlying structure we talked about is similar to the phenomenon of *an echo.* A sound is made; it hits a "sounding board" and the sound reverberates and comes back to us. The nature of the sounding board will surely affect the reverberation. In the same way, an event happens; it strikes something within us and we get a feeling. What was struck resounds within us, there at the median layer of emotion where the two poles of Life-Love and Death are anchored. If the echo is an "enlivening" emotion we can determine that the incident touched the source of Life and Love within us, and awakened the Spirit joined to our spirit. (Rom 8: 16) If the feeling response can be named a "stifling" emotion, then this indicates that the event has called out to that susceptibility in us that is always ready to lead us to Death.

Therefore, it is very important to be aware of our feelings in any situation whether we are reflecting or praying about some decision by ourselves, making a choice that involves another person or a group decision, or simply taken up by the ordinary events of our lives. The "enlivening" or "stifling" taste of our emotions discloses to us that, in our depths, we feel good, secure, and energized — or insecure, threatened, and endangered.

When I want to check out with my heart the appropriateness of what my head has done, I simply have to apply what we have just explained. In other words, I take the solution that my intellect has proposed and, taking my time, I let it sink in. I meditate and contemplate, ruminate and pray with it and about it. The longer I stay with that solution, the more sensitive I may become to what I feel about it. The more clearly I will be able to hear the echo of its impact at the very bottom of my heart. It might take quite a while before the particular tone of my feeling is clear. That depends on the gravity of the question, the quality of my intellectual work, how much and how often I am able to brood over the possible solution, to what degree my daily occupations distract me from pondering.

But, at some point in time, I will be able to say to myself, "The longer I weigh this option, the better (or the worse) I feel about it." At that moment I can say that my sensitivity to Life and Love, to the Spirit of Agape within me, responded to my inquiry about the appropriateness of this solution for me. On the other hand, I might have to say that it was my susceptibility to deadly tendencies that replied to my question.

If we remember that it is never possible to be a hundred percent certain, we may say: The solution proposed by my head provokes "enlivening" feelings at the deeper levels of my heart, either always or more and more consistently. In that case it is very probable that my most intimate being, united to the Spirit of Life and Love within me, is at peace and rejoices with the prospect of accepting this proposal. My inner being is pleased with what "pleases the Lord." (Ep 5: 10)

If, on the contrary, I experience "stifling" feelings, either always or more and more consistently, it is very likely that the solution I chose, transformed into a decision and acted upon, will only increase and feed my deadly tendencies. These have nothing to do with God's Spirit.

So, I let the "intellectual" solution call to my depths and I listen to the sound of the echo and its impact. The more consistently the resounding is in a minor key, the more accurately this tells me that my depths and the Spirit lament. A more consistent major-key response reveals that my heart and the Spirit exult. Spiritual authors have called these phenomena *desolation* and *consolation*.

If just the prospect of choosing the solution resulting from my intellectual activity gives me such feelings, how much more so will the decision once it is acted upon. It is very important, then, to heed the warning I receive in discernment. Making a decision while what I am pondering as an option is creating "stifling" feelings can only be damaging to me, and the fear that I would be devastated by carrying out such a decision for any length of time would be justified. Sure, it might be my decision, but, in the end, it might be my death. We have all watched people get into deep trouble by forcing themselves to make and to adhere to a decision that was not in tune with their depth.

On the other hand, when I decide to choose the solution that has been evoking "enlivening" feelings throughout my decision-making process, and when I act out my choice, what was budding there during discernment will blossom. It is really my decision, and each step of its concrete realization will make me more alive and loving, bearing more fruit in Agape. Examples abound of people blooming in their deeds, a sure sign that their choice was a good one for them.

Therefore, the conclusion is clear: The intellectual solution that brings *me* desolation is not *for me*. It may fit someone else but, at this time of my life, it is not for me. The option that creates consolation in *me* is really the one *for me*. Other people may not agree, but they do not have *my* heart.

Verifying with our heart is following the teaching of John, "Beloved, do not trust every spirit, but put the spirits to a test to see if they belong to God." (1 Jn 4: 1) In this instance the Apostle is referring to false prophets but, even within us, we don't have to accept false voices and we must reject any voice that is not from God's Spirit.

Once the decision has been made and we throw ourselves into acting upon it, we become the witnesses of the words of Jesus, "A good tree does not produce decayed fruit any more than a decayed tree produces good fruit ... Someone who is good produces goodness from the good of his heart; an evil person produces evil out of his store of evil." (Lk 6: 43, 45)

PAINFUL LIFE-GIVING CHOICES; EASY BUT HURTFUL DECISIONS

If we look back over our lives, we may not always be able to agree with some of the assertions made in the last pages. We have all had the experience of making a decision while feeling somewhat uncomfortable about it, and time has proven that it was good for us. At other times, we may have started to act upon a decision that we had felt good about and the result of our action was catastrophic!

—— I was so pleased with my decision to spend a few weeks of
vacation with some friends of mine; those days turned out
to be a disaster.
—— It was very hard to leave my family and my country. But
after a time my decision to serve the poor in Africa filled
my heart with peace and joy.

These experiences may seem to negate what was said in
previous chapters. In fact, they are usually the consequences of
a more complex process, and this has to be explained. In such
cases discernment needs to be refined.

"DIFFICULT" FEELINGS, "HAPPY ENDING"

In general, whenever we experience "stifling" feelings while
working with our affectivity on our intellectual solution, it is
better for us not to choose this course of action for it will lead
us to a dead end, literally. However, it sometimes happens that,
dealing with the product of our intellect, we feel some *apparently* "stifling" emotions. We may feel troubled or saddened,
tepid or apathetic, hopeless or faithless, lazy or resistant, restless or mournful, fearful or in dread, for example. Is this real
desolation?

I have frequently encountered people who were in this
predicament, dealing with something difficult to accept. Often
their comments could be summarized in the words of one of
them, "I feel I have to face that." Were they hypnotized by
death, as we all can be when we are trapped by our masochism?
I would say no. Actually they impressed me as being not
masochists but fighters, resolved to confront the adversary, or
wrestlers, determined to struggle with their opponent courageously. In fact, their desire to fight sounded "hopeful."

In the context of a directed retreat, I have often suggested
that someone in these straits go forward, living with the problem, checking it out in order to see what time would reveal. If it
appeared, in time, that the person were on a deadly journey, my
advice would be to stop everything and reconsider the question. However, for some people, after a while the thick fog dis-

sipated and, in the light, we discovered that the person was not being led to a dead end. We saw that the situation was a kind of *Passover* experience, the beginning of an Exodus toward life.

It's true that sometimes we have to confront very harsh circumstances and, when we do so, we experience, let us say, "difficult" feelings, the kind we usually connect with death. These feelings are appropriate because what we are facing is, indeed, a temporary death. But it is in order to enter into a new life: we are crossing the Red Sea, we live the Paschal mystery of Christ.

—— I remember a man who was painfully confronting his mother's death. It was time for him to pass through a new birth canal, cut the umbilical cord, and become an adult.
—— Another person faced a problem with a difficult superior. In order to be free he needed to learn to say "no," to risk displeasing people, and it was causing him anguish.
—— A woman debated whether or not to remain a member of her religious community. By passing through the fear of leaving what was, for her, a cocoon, and the dread of entering a "dangerous world," she discovered a lay person's way of living the same spirituality.
—— A friend of mine, a supervisor, had to risk her own job by firing an employee. She crossed the sea of her anxieties and found herself at one with her evangelical values.

Thomas Aquinas, in the thirteenth century, said, "The real good angels sometimes frighten people by their coming, but their presence very quickly becomes a source of consolation and strength." There are truly difficult feelings that accompany the experience of death and resurrection in the depth of our being. Life and Love call us to freedom, but Passion is the door to Resurrection. Accepting pruning and trimming in order to increase our yield and bear new fruit is never an easy task. (Jn 15: 2) Called to leave what possesses us and follow Agape can create some sadness in us, but, "if by the Spirit, you put to death the evil deeds of the body, you will live," guarantees Paul. (Mk 10: 22; Rom 8: 13) How can we expect to avoid difficult feelings when we know the agony of Jesus in our life? (Mk 10: 32–40) In those moments, we need to allow the faith of Paul to support our own: "If the Spirit of God who raised Jesus from the dead dwells in you, then God who raised Christ from the dead will bring your mortal bodies to life also, through the Spirit dwelling in you." (Rom 8: 11)

Perhaps the faint echo of hope perceptible in the desire to stay with it reached by the people I just described was already a sign that the Spirit was not lamenting. Maybe it resulted from a very fleeting glimpse of the distant bank of the Red Sea. It may have been the indistinct refrain of a hymn of victory, in the words of Dietrich Bonhoeffer, "a victory already won."

"ENJOYABLE" FEELINGS, "CRASH LANDING"

We have also had the experience of feeling really good about a possible solution and deciding to go ahead based on that feeling. The fruit may have had a delicious taste at first but then began to go sour, going from bad to worse until, in the end, we were left looking in amazement at the bitter pit.

We could all narrate minor (or major) tragedies that resemble the ones I have summarized here:

—— I have a bitter argument with my brother. Resolved to initiate a reconciliation, I go back to him. The quarrel we get into this time is worse than the first.
—— I decide joyfully to visit my in-laws because they are alone. Picturing myself giving them joy, I let them complain about their financial troubles. Soon, talking about taxes leads us into a heated argument about politics. A hostile silence ensues and the evening is totally ruined.
—— We want to provide a good life for our children. We buy a new and larger house, new furniture, etc. Soon the bills start piling up and this means extra hours of work to pay them. We are home less and less and become more and more irritable. Our family life deteriorates.
—— A man joins the army because of his ideals. In wartime he

sees himself forced, in spite of his personal ethics and his religious belief, to accept the fact that prisoners are being tortured to get information. He is deeply damaged within himself.

These stories talk about a deviation of trajectory. The process usually starts with a generous and noble project. Affectively it has been decided upon with good feelings such as happiness and courage, joy or strength, hope and peace. Was this real consolation? The end result was a disaster! It's like a rocket heading for the moon that turns and eventually crashes in the ocean. The trajectory has been diverted.

Each time we have to deal with authorities, every time we are with someone of the opposite sex, whenever a question of money is raised, in every group situation, when we have to deal with an employee — the occasion is different for each one of us — it seems we cannot avoid the same unhappy development. It's as if a *pattern* exists that we never clearly perceive. Eventually, after some very painful experiences in similar circumstances, we hear ourselves saying, "That's the last time I talk about politics with my in-laws," or "Honey, from now on you deal with the kids about school," or "I'm never going to get involved with the women in my office again."

This kind of decision, or resignation, shows that we have finally become aware that something was radically wrong for us in that kind of scene. We realize that it was wrong right from the start, and that the unwinding of the film always revealed the same unhappy ending in those circumstances. We sense a mechanism we cannot control once it has been put into motion. The ordinary insight that we all have that enables us to recognize, even if we are still unable to analyze, what is happening in these cases is the same wisdom of the spiritual authors of years ago, who named the experience, "When the evil one transforms himself into an angel of light."

When we read 1 Kings and 2 Chronicles, we start out admiring Solomon's wisdom and his dedication as he builds God's house in fulfillment of a promise made by David, his father. But, as the chapters unfold, the beautiful image that we have of such a master in terms of discernment becomes tarnished by his sins. And, eventually we begin to ask, "Was the Temple really built to honor God, or in order to centralize everything in Jerusalem so that the king might have the power and the glory?" Historians confirm our suspicions: an apparent religious zeal cloaks an ambitious man.

Apparent generosity, gentleness, dedication, or zeal can mask other motivations that are less noble. Aren't we generous sometimes because we want to call attention to ourselves or because we do not want to be rejected? Can our gentleness be a way to seduce or manipulate people? And as for our dedication, can't this be a ploy we use to win admiration or to find ourselves worthy of congratulations? Our zeal may simply be an insurance against insecurity: we try to convince others of our own ideas so that we may feel certain, superior, or powerful.

When we stop fooling ourselves, we know that our *best* desires and projects might be servants of our deepest selfishness. And then, through our apparent generosity and noble ambitions, we are caught in what might be called the traps of dedication. "We are made sinners," said Paul in Romans, and he does not put any qualifications on that name by saying, "except in this or that." (5: 19) The susceptibility to death affects everything within us, and *even our love is not immune from temptation and sin.* A great step forward in the spiritual life is taken when we understand that nothing is pure in a sinful human being and when we acknowledge that everything has to be saved — has been saved in Jesus Christ.

Let us not forget that there were some Pharisees so zealous for God's Law that they did not recognize God's Son. Paul, because of his "excess of zeal" became "a blasphemer, a persecutor." (1 Tm 1: 13; Ga 1: 13–14; Acts 9; 22; 26) Peter and Judas dedicated themselves to Jesus, but denied and betrayed him. And Jesus himself was "tempted by the devil" through apparently good thoughts: eating because he was hungry, believing that angels would protect him as God's Son. But it did not work as it does in our case, for Christ knew too well the "father of lies." (Mt 4; Jn 8: 44)

Again, quoting Aquinas, "The false good angels, that means the devils, though they start by exciting people toward what is good, soon alter their language and quickly lead them to evil." To borrow an explanation from Ignatius, a master in spirituality and discernment, we can describe the process of deviation of trajectory like this:

> It is characteristic of the evil one to transform himself into an angel of light, to work with the soul in the beginning but, in the end, to work for himself. At first he will suggest good and holy thoughts that are in conformity with the disposition of a just soul, then, little by little, he strives to gain his own ends by drawing the soul into his hidden deceits and perverse designs.
>
> (*The Spiritual Exercises*, 332)

Our inner wounds are always there consistently provoking us to act for our self-satisfaction or preservation. Sometimes we envision some action where both of these self-centered urges can find gratification; that is probably why we have such good feelings at the beginning. So, we decide and we act accordingly. But the rocket very quickly veers off course, in spite of the beautiful goal we had in mind. Our gut betrays our head. To the degree that the situation we have put ourselves in feeds our selfishness, the distortions become more and more apparent. When we finally become aware of what is going on, it may be too late.

The "father of lies" has gotten his way by playing upon our inability to be separate from or to tolerate intimacy with our childhood rival, for example. Or by tapping into our desire to please that cannot be thwarted. Or by appealing to our desire for a protective cocoon at all cost. Or by flattering our macho image, which is a stronger motivation than our ethical values.

It would be helpful if it were possible to make an in-flight correction of our rocket's deviation!

Peter probably felt very content with himself, confident about his spiritual insight, when Jesus praised him for his confession, "You are the Messiah." Did Peter begin to imagine his career as a spiritual writer? When he decided to "remonstrate" with Jesus because of the announcement of the Passion, the Master immediately perceived the "satan" there and corrected the deviation. (Mt 16: 13–23) It would be extremely helpful to have someone always at hand who could prevent us from taking the wrong direction, but, most of the time, this is our own affair. What can we do to correct our own flight pattern?

Rockets usually maintain their course because of computer programming. We need to use the technology of our intellect and affectivity.

First with our head, let us pinpoint in what circumstances and with which people we are often trapped by a dangerous generosity. It may be that this always occurs when we are teaching or when we are assisting, when we are in a group of peers or with our competitors, etc. Awareness of the entrapping environment will help us to prepare ourselves, at least, to respond more appropriately the next time we are in a similar situation, for some situations occur fairly regularly in our lives.

But how we choose to act the next time will depend, also, on our recognition of the different steps in the development of the pattern. Following the advice of Ignatius of Loyola again, let us analyze the process step by step, looking for each turning point, working backward from the end of the flight to the beginning. (*The Spiritual Exercises,* 333–334) It is easier to start from the end because the final twists and turns are the most extreme and, consequently, the most apparent. The very first distortions were probably so subtle and unconscious as to be barely noticeable. If we had been able to perceive them at that point, it might have been possible to get right back on course or to manage the moments that followed our deviation in quite another way.

May I take the case of my visit with my in-laws, for example? I put the tape of our dialogue on "rewind," listening to the topics in reverse change from presidential candidates to political parties to tax gripes to financial worries. I listen as well to the volume of our voices that diminishes in decibels as we approach the start of the tape. In this way I act as the observer of the gradual destruction of the evening.

Plotting each point of the skewed course is the work of the intellect.

After this procedure, I do the same thing with my heart. Remembering what happened, and still moving backward, I try to locate the moments when my feelings began to change for the worse. Using the example of my evening with my in-laws, I feel myself moving back from bursting with rage through hot under the collar, through slightly aggravated and edgy, right back to calm and somewhat neutral. I can easily trace the deterioration of my gut reactions. By conducting our own investigation in this way, we begin to see how our inner susceptibility gets caught up in a vicious and deadly whirlpool.

Later, if we find ourselves in the middle of similar circumstances, we will be able to hear our intellect and our affectivity blowing the whistle and sounding the alarm when we reach and recognize the different danger signs discovered previously by our human tools of mind and heart. Thus, we'll be able to make better decisions, accepting our Passovers or escaping entrapping circumstances.

Struggling with Ambiguity

It should be obvious now why this section should start with the statement, "discernment needs to be refined." In both kinds of cases described above it is necessary. When we have "difficult" feelings our first tendency might be to draw back, to flee; when our emotions are taking us on an "enjoyable" ride we might feel urged to rush into things. In either case we might miss out on the new life offered to us or find ourselves even more engulfed in our deadly dispositions. It would be better to discern carefully in order to avoid delusional escapes or painful awakenings. Practicing discernment through light and darkness will obviously take time, but it will also teach us something about ourselves and permit us to create over time reflexes and management skills that will be very fruitful for our future, fruitful in terms of Life and Love. Isn't it true that when we love someone we delight in training ourselves to become more and more sensitive? We must remember that the soloist's composure as well as his achievement is the fruit of hours of practice.

The process of refining our discernment helps us to grow in the realistic understanding that everything in our human existence — including love — is characterized by *ambiguity*. Surely, when a person leaps out in front of a car to save a child heedlessly crossing the street, we may suspect the presence of Agape with a minimum of interference from self-centered motivation. But most of our important decisions are not a struggle-free business, because things are rarely crystal clear.

We do not like ambiguity because it condemns everything: even our noblest desires probably have selfish roots. But we forget that ambiguity also saves everything: nothing in our lives is perfectly evil. Ambiguity condemns the best and saves the worst. Of course, accepting ambiguity and laboring for discernment is a struggle for us. After all, Jesus warned us saying, "Do not suppose that my mission on earth is to spread peace ..." (Mt 10: 34–36) He graphically described divisions in a family, but what household is more intimate to us than our own depths? When making a decision is very difficult, we may remember that "From John the Baptizer's time until now the Kingdom of God has suffered violence, and the violent take it by force." (Mt 11: 12) Sometimes discernment is truly our acceptance of that "violence." With that kind of surgery we are going to be less and less blind. With purified eyes, according to one of the Beatitudes, we shall see God in our life, in our lifetime. (Mt 5: 8)

The whole process that we undertake with our affectivity can be summarized in this chart:

		EXTERIORLY	
		IN A SITUATION THAT REQUIRES THE USUAL DISCERNMENT	IN A SITUATION THAT REQUIRES A REFINED DISCERNMENT
I N T E R I O R L Y	OUR SENSITIVITY TO LIFE AND LOVE RESPONDS BY ⟶	1. "Enlivening" feelings that last.	3. "Difficult" feelings apparently "stifling." (Replaced by 1. when the new life appears.)
	OUR SUSCEPTIBILITY TO DEATH REACTS WITH ⟶	2. "Stifling" feelings that last.	4. "Enjoyable" feelings apparently "enlivening." (Replaced by 2. when the end of the process is approaching and arrives.)

3

How to Become
Freer from the
Beginning

AN EXPERT'S POINT OF VIEW

Is what we have already considered all there is to it? Do we now have a method of discernment in its entirety? Let us compare what we now have in our hands with what an expert teaches us about the same subject. We go to Ignatius of Loyola (1491–1556), the founder of the Society of Jesus, who is an acknowledged discernment specialist in the Christian tradition. In *The Spiritual Exercises*, which is a manual for the ones who help people make their own decisions through directed retreats, Ignatius very carefully describes, in the language of his century, several methods of decision making. The method he dwells on at length includes six points or steps:

1. The first point is to place before my mind's eye the thing on [sic] which I wish to make a choice. It may be an office or a benefice to be accepted or refused, or anything else that is the object of a mutable choice.

2. I must have as my aim the end for which I was created, which is the praise of God our Lord and the salvation of my soul. At the same time I must remain indifferent and free of any inordinate attachments so that I am not more inclined or disposed to take the

thing proposed or to reject it, nor to relinquish it rather than to accept it. I must rather be like the equalized scales of balance, ready to follow the course which I feel is more for the glory and praise of God our Lord and the salvation of my soul.

3. I must ask God our Lord to deign to move my will and reveal to my spirit what I should do to best promote His praise and glory in the matter of choice. After examining the matter thoroughly and faithfully with my understanding, I should make my choice in conformity with His good pleasure and His most holy will.

4. I will use my reason to weigh the many advantages and benefits that would accrue to me if I held the proposed office or benefice solely for the praise of God our Lord and the salvation of my soul. I will likewise consider and weigh the disadvantages and the dangers that there are in holding it. I will proceed in like manner with the other alternative, that is, examine and consider the advantages and benefits as well as the disadvantages and dangers in not holding the proposed office or benefice.

5. After having thus weighed the matter and carefully examined it from every side, I will consider which alternative appears to be more reasonable. Acting upon the stronger judgment of reason and not on any inclination of the senses I must come to a decision in the matter that I am considering.

6. After such a choice or decision has been reached, I should turn with great diligence to prayer in the presence of God our Lord and offer him this choice that his Divine Majesty may deign to accept and confirm it, if it be to his greater service and praise. (pp. 85–86)*

---

* I use the translation of Anthony Mottola, Image Books, Doubleday and Company, Inc. Garden City, New York, 1964.

Even though the language used is from another century, we can easily recognize many ideas treated earlier in this book that were in fact inspired by *The Spiritual Exercises*. In the first paragraph we see posed the problem of a choice, the same kind of choice we have been dealing with from the beginning of this book.

It is good to remind ourselves through this point, that it is necessary, from the very first, to formulate a clear idea of the exact nature of the object of our choice. As long as that object is not clearly perceived, the time is not ripe for making a decision.*

In the third, fourth, and fifth points we find different expressions of what we have been calling the work of our intellect. "With my *understanding*" (3) "I will use my *reason*" (4) "... which alternative appears more *reasonable* ... acting upon the stronger *judgment of reason*" (5), are all expressions that describe the activity of the intellect.

In our text, we have interpreted the Ignatian language of "advantages and benefits, disadvantages and dangers" (4), by using the image of the potential steps forward or backward that we can see represented by our alternatives. We might also have expressed this by asking ourselves, "Which solution will give me the advantage of taking one more step toward Agape? Which solution will be a disadvantage and dangerous because it leads to Death?" But, I use the words I have chosen for two reasons. In current usage, "advantages and disadvantages, benefits and dangers" can be easily interpreted as promoting selfishness. Labeling this step "weighing the pros and cons" is not satisfactory either, since it tends to depersonalize the examination and leads me to make a very generalized evaluation of alternatives that has little to do with "the one I am." For, even though I need my intellect to be as ob-

---

*See the Appendix entitled *What Can We Do to Clarify the Object of the Choice?*

jective as possible, I must still do the work with my own mind, not someone's else.

When Ignatius says, "… to best promote His praise and glory in the matter of choice … in conformity with His good pleasure and His … holy will …" (3), he expresses within a Christian context and in the language of that century, what we intend by considering our options in the light of our faith and our values.

I mentioned earlier in this text that one of the ways in which our intellect learns about faith is through prayer. The same recognition, this same understanding, is implied in the urging of Ignatius, "I must ask God our Lord to deign … to reveal to my spirit what I should do …" (3).

For those who are familiar with Ignatian terms, it is easy to recognize in the sixth point the process described in the section of this text entitled *How to Listen to My Heart*. When Ignatius counsels us to offer the decision to God, "that His Divine Majesty may deign to accept and confirm it," he means that, if the choice is the right one, he expects to experience consolation ("enlivening" feelings). As we have seen, it signifies that the heart and the Spirit exult and agree, "accept and confirm" the option proposed by the intellect. This, of course, implies that if we have made a poor choice desolation will occur with "stifling" feelings, and we must repeat the process to see where we have made a mistake.

INDIFFERENCE

So, the only point of the method of Ignatius not mentioned so far in this book is the second one that concerns the notion of *indifference*. It is necessary to clarify this concept, which has been a very essential subject for spiritual authors for centuries. The meaning they gave to the term might not occur to us today. We are more likely now to use this word to lament a certain insensitivity, a lack of concern, an apathetic or lukewarm attitude. But we can find alternate definitions in our dictionaries:

absence of compulsion toward one thing or another, for example, or, in the case of the adjective "indifferent," marked by no special liking for or dislike of something, marked by no special preference for one thing or another. In Ignatius' day and age, and in the writings of other spiritual authors, this latter meaning was the sense intended, with an emphasis on a freedom that was not hindered by the influence of affective reactions, our "passions," in their words.

Probably the best way to express the concept of indifference in modern terms would be to say *inner freedom.*

So, reaching the point of indifference means no longer being enslaved or led by any strong interior impulse or attraction toward any of the alternatives presented by our mind in the decision process. Our predecessors, in their wisdom and through their experience, knew that choosing implied responsibility and freedom; they had already discovered that, so long as one was not free within oneself but ruled by one's "passions," it would be impossible to assert that the decision to come would be the result of a free choice. They had already perceived what modern psychologists have clearly explained in other words: that, often, hidden motives are so forceful in persuading us to do one thing or another that we cannot claim that we have chosen. We were not free. We saw the best examples of that lack of freedom in what I called deviation of trajectory based on "enjoyable" feelings.

How can we follow the advice of Ignatius, then, given in his second point? Including time in any process of discernment already frees us from any impulsive tendency to solve our question too quickly — at least when life allows us to do that. But the problem is to try to become freer from the beginning.

ESTABLISHING FREEDOM AS A STARTING POINT

Contrary to the myth of rationality, as we have already discussed, the head cannot be separated from the heart. This is a truth expressed in the Old Testament when the writers saw the heart as the location of both understanding and feeling. In order to simplify the description of the process of discernment, while talking about the work of the intellect I chose not to dwell on that fact. But when our head is at work, it cannot avoid being influenced by our gut. Therefore, the objective analysis and its result are actually far from being objective. We are all familiar with what psychologists call rationalization. It is a kind of intellectual discourse that goes on in us when we cover up or justify subconscious motives that are irrational. My gut rents the services of my head in order to get what it wants by presenting logical and credible reasons for acting. The sharper my head, the more sophisticated and convincing the pros and cons will look to other people, as well as to myself.

Thus, in what seems like a free and responsible decision, we can be ruled by our phobias or obsessions, by our inferiority complex or our anguish, by our perverse phantasms or our inclination to sadism, by our masochism or our childish submission, etc. It is no surprise, then, that a decision made under these influences and put into action eventually leads to catastrophe.

Therefore, when we have a decision to make, it would be better *to start* the very decision-making process by trying to become freer, as Ignatius suggests. We would be able then to work with an intellect that would not be the lackey of orientations already determined beneath the surface. What can liberate us?

THE STRONGEST POSSIBLE MOTIVATION

We have recalled the word *passions* used by spiritual authors in the past because it will be useful here. In order to reach the point of indifference, we are advised to seek liberation from the *passions* that dwell within us. *Only a passion can overcome another passion.*

Hate or Love, for instance, have made many people strong enough to fight and master compulsions that were anchored in their being. Terrorists, who were blasted away by the bomb they carried in a plane, overcame the natural instinct of survival and the normal concern for innocent bystanders by their fanatic religious or political passion. I have known some alcoholic people who have overcome their addiction to drinking by their passionate love for their spouse and children.

If we want to journey toward inner freedom, it is necessary to start with the energy found in a passion stronger than the other ones, in a passion taken to its most absolute and radical level. That is why Ignatius advises the person of his time who wants to make an important decision, to start by facing his or her human vocation. He says, "I must have as my aim the end for which I am created, which is the praise of God our Lord and the salvation of my soul ... [I must be] ... ready to follow the course which I feel is more for the glory and praise of God our Lord and the salvation of my soul." (2) For a Christian of that period, nothing could be more powerful than the two goals mentioned by Ignatius.

Following the same logic, I opened the chapter *How to Work with My Head,* by reminding ourselves of our call by Agape, our call to choose Agape and not Death. If we are believers, we cannot find anything more important, motivating, and energizing, for our most terrible tragedy would be to be away from God, Love and Life in Person. The stake here is really the ultimate one. In the case of nonbelievers, the process is very much the same: they have to face the supreme values they believe in and cherish the most, in order to make a choice that will not be a betrayal. It is an undeniable fact that many men and women have been so convinced of the preciousness of their values that they became free — even to the point of accepting the loss of their life in an astounding witness of indifference.

How much more would a passionate love for God, who loved so much in Jesus Christ, be able to liberate Christians. More than any value, this love can mobilize us, increase our strength, and overcome our other passions. At the very least, in front of God's being and call, everything else is put in the right perspective and takes on its proper dimensions.

Speaking of this, we cannot help but recall Paul's logic in his Letter to the Colossians. The Apostle reminds his readers that, being baptized, they are already in Christ, in God's love. He wonders, therefore, why they would be interested in things that have less or no value. Based on this, Paul gives and justifies his ascetical message and teaching, not as a goal in itself, *but as a consequence*; love leads us easily to accept sacrifices for others, while making sacrifices might be in itself just another way of being self-centered.

Thus, through reflection and prayer, we begin working *on our affectivity*, so that we can free ourselves of the emotional charge of the issue we face that stirs up within us the forces of the gut, that might otherwise take control of us and rule us without our real consent. How can we recognize that we have reached the point of indifference? What are the signs?

BALANCE

Ignatius paints us a picture of indifference, "I must rather be like the equalized scales of balance." The image of the scale that the statue of Justice holds in her hands is perhaps the best way to describe what people who try to become indifferent experience. After fluctuating for a while between their spontaneous attraction to this and their natural repulsion for that, the mechanism of balance tends to stabilize.

It is important to remember that, although we hope for the moment when the scales are balanced, the period of experiencing fluctuation and vacillation (and indecisiveness) is far from being shameful and wasted. It is even necessary. It is only by fully accepting and attending to my ups and downs, my wavering, that I will eventually be able to recognize the still point of my internal mechanism, the point at which the two scales rest motionless.

At that time, we may hear the person saying, "This alternative or that? It does not really matter as long as ... I am with the Lord." Nonbelievers might say, "as long as I can be honest, as long as the members of my family still love each other, as long as I have good health, as long as the poor are served," etc. This would entirely depend on each individual's personal system of values and convictions. If perfect indifference is impossible, we can reach a level of inner liberty compatible with freedom and responsibility.

When the process has worked well, and the inner struggle and oscillation is over, the person is inhabited by the quiet and peaceful feeling of no longer being fascinated or hypnotized by one of the alternatives, of no longer being particularly attracted by either side of the choice. Ignatius himself uses a vocabulary that implies feeling, for he says, "inclined" or "disposed"; and in another famous section of the *Exercises* he speaks of indifference saying, "… we should not *prefer* health to sickness, riches to poverty, honor to dishonor, a long life to a short one, and so in all things we should *desire* and choose only those things which will best help us to attain the end for which we were created." (Italics mine, pp. 47–48) When he describes the state of mind and heart we need to experience he calls it "a time of tranquility." (pp. 84–85)

The description given here, as well as the words of Ignatius, clearly shows that such inner freedom has nothing to do with insensitivity or unconcern, carelessness or apathy. It is far from being a lukewarm attitude; in fact, it is quite the opposite. In the words of a friend of mine, "When people reach indifference, it is because of a preference" — a prior and stronger preference. "Because I prefer the good of my family above all, I have quit smoking, drinking, or gambling …." As Christians, we are invited to prefer Agape first of all — the same Life and Love we read about in Deuteronomy 30. It is the "God first served" of Joan of Arc. At the same time it is the accomplishment of our lives as sons and daughters of the Lord ("the salvation of my soul," said Ignatius and his contemporaries), and it is the well-being of the brothers and sisters we serve.

The fact that indifference is rooted in a preference implies that it is grounded in readiness. The person who is truly indifferent is ready to use the means, take the way most suitable to

Agape — the ways and the means that are not opposed to the ultimate goal. "I must rather be like the equalized scales of balance, *ready* to follow the course which I feel is more for the glory and praise of God ...." (Italics mine)

I know that I have reached indifference when I hear myself saying, "This road or that one, it does not matter to me, as long as I am in Agape. I am just waiting for a signal and I'll go." This is the time to start working with my head and my heart on my decision. At this point I am liberated enough, free enough to be able to perceive the signs that my intellect and my affectivity will give me while I am using the method described here.

THE NEED FOR TIME AND GRACE

Usually we think that the decision itself is the difficulty. But such is not the case. What is most difficult is to become free. As an example of that, in a thirty-day retreat Ignatius starts talking about the possibility of making a choice only after two full weeks of preparation. We need time because indifference is difficult to acquire. It takes time to perceive our "passions" and to let them calm down. We need time to become aware of our subconscious motivations and see them losing power. If I repeat "indifferent *enough*" so often, it is because perfect indifference is very probably impossible for us. All our limitations hinder us in the attainment of perfect inner liberty. One meaning of *enough* here is that we are at least conscious of our spontaneous attractions and repulsions at the beginning of the discernment process. And we are willing to look at them carefully and, at the minimum, proceed with caution. We have already seen in a previous chapter how some of our spontaneous attractions concealed a trap and how some natural resistances hid a positive call. *Enough* also means that we have been able to get some distance from our impulses and find ourselves more capable of recovering our inner freedom.

But enough is never enough! So we must use the only tool we have left for becoming indifferent: we need to beg the perfectly free One to give us this grace. It is there that prayer plays its most important role in this process. We pray, we beseech God to help us, as so many people did with Jesus. We humbly pray to the Lord, who hears the cry of the poor. For nonbelievers, this would mean summoning up within themselves the very incarnation of their most precious values.

It's so difficult to become free that the effort to remain indifferent must be present throughout the discernment process and so, too, the permanent prayer for the grace of freedom. In fact, this is precisely why Ignatius sends people back to God at the end of the process by having them offer their decision. (6) It is never certain that somewhere along the way, very surreptitiously, a lack of indifference has not crept back in. That's also the reason why we put the work of affectivity after the work of the intellect in this book. This not only enables us to determine whether the solution of our mind is acceptable to our heart, but it also helps us to find out if we have been indifferent enough during the process to assure that our decision conforms to Agape dwelling in the depths of our being.

LOVE AS OUR PREFERENCE

Some of us wonder if it is really worthwhile to take so much time and to make such an effort when we are making a decision. We need to take our precious time because human life is priceless. If we are deciding to get married or to remain single, let's take the time. When we are going to make a change in our firm that will affect 20 or 10,000 employees, it's worth our time. If we plan to conclude an agreement that concerns millions of citizens or make a ruling that binds all the faithful — both merit time. Reforming a school system that will forge the minds and the hearts of our children requires time.

Even when the issues involved do not have the scope of the ones we just mentioned, they are still important. We will want to take time for discernment so that we will be accustomed to the method and prepared to use it when we have a serious matter to decide. It is Jesus who tells us, "The one who can be trusted in little things can be trusted in great; the one who is dishonest in little things will be dishonest in great." (Lk 16: 10) A thoughtful love does not consider anything too small, too unimportant. Everything is an equal opportunity for showing love. Such a delicate sense of love knows that little things can hurt badly, that love does not calculate but tries to be fully present in any event. Spouses and friends understand this.

Of course, when we have an emergency situation with little time for reflection, we must do what we can. But the practice we have had in using the method can give us the reflexes to make the best possible choice under the circumstances.

Ultimately, the appeal to take the time and the pain to discern comes from a very deep place. It is given definition in our desire to see Agape more fully present in this world through our own life and activity. We may recall the regret of Teresa of Avila, "What is sad is that Love is not loved." If we love enough to want Love manifested, recognized, and accepted, it is given expression in our actions, and the clarity of our acts depends on the lucidity of our discernment.

As believers, can we see the lesson that so many nonbelievers, dedicated to justice, peace, and human rights, for example, give us? Would we do less? Would we refuse to take the time and devote the labor for discernment, we who say every day, "Hallowed be thy name; thy kingdom come," to the One we call Agape?

4

We Are "Servants Put in Charge"

In the last chapter I pointed out that we are in charge of our individual decisions. God treats us as responsible servants. Therefore at the end of this part about individual discernment, we can answer one question that is frequently asked, and offer one possible description of spiritual growth.

GOD'S WILL

Often people ask the question, "What is God's will for me?" It is as if somewhere, outside themselves, God had already determined everything, drawn a map that delimited their precise itinerary, or drafted a blueprint that depicted the plan of their lives. If it were so, our freedom would be only an appearance. It would be like the freedom of a child who says yes to his parents' decisions about a trip without having been a responsible partner in the choice of the route and the destination. It would be only half a freedom because it would be merely the liberty to discover and accept something already decided by someone else. God does not make half-gifts: we have been made really free.

Obviously, human life is bounded by unavoidable limitations that preclude perfect freedom. But it is *our* business to carve out our own paths within the boundaries of our life situations, in a responsible manner and with God's help. Then what does it mean to talk about God's will for us? As many scholars said long ago, let us assert that *God's will is our will.* That may sound paradoxical but the preceding chapters suggest that this is true, once we descend to the level we have described.

Within ourselves, by the process of discernment we offer the results of our intellectual search to the Spirit; if our Divine Guest indicates agreement with us through enlivening echoes produced at the core of our being, we may say that, at that level, we and the Spirit are in tune with one another, that we are deciding *together* our will. What we want at this depth is what God wants for us: God's will for us is what we decide.

It is true that in a general way, we are all "predestined through Christ Jesus to be adopted sons" and daughters, as we read in Ephesians. (1: 5) However, through the process of discernment we verify with the Spirit what we have discovered with our intellect and affectivity. "The Spirit himself gives witness with our spirit," and both of us define which *specific* son or daughter we are impelled to become in the here and now. (Rom 8: 16)

Spiritual Growth in Three Words

Practicing discernment, whether in big or small decisions, gives us the opportunity of developing more systematically potentialities we all have because the faculty of reasoning and feeling is a human gift. And we enjoy the benefit of working as responsible adults with the Spirit. But we also develop the knowledge of what spiritual growth is about. This can be summed up in three words: *awareness, sensitivity,* and *management.*

AWARENESS

It is by growing accustomed to using the tools of discernment that we deepen our self-knowledge. We progressively discover more about our wounds, our weaknesses and strengths, our tendencies and their impact on our lives. We can paint a more accurate portrait of ourselves showing all the bright and the dark, as well as the gray features. We become more aware of who we are.

Simultaneously we acquire a clearer knowledge of our own God. What does that mean? The four Evangelists believed in the same Christ but each one described him according to his personal perception. In the same way, it is because of who I am that I am able to see more and more lucidly the "particular" God that attracts me. It may be truer to say that God, knowing the kind of person I am, reveals a face that will charm me, as Jeremiah said. (20: 7) If I am an orphan, for instance, I might be touched by a God who never abandons anyone. If I am an outcast I may feel a kinship with the One crucified outside of the walls of Jerusalem. If I see myself as an "ordinary person" I might cherish the unknown carpenter of Nazareth. And each new experience we have verifies, clarifies, and deepens our awareness about our "name" and the name of our God.

SENSITIVITY

It is the same for us: the more we become conscious of our own identity, the sooner we can recognize in each situation what will favor our Life or our Death. Discernment has developed our "sixth" sense: this trained intuition enables some of us, for instance, to detect injustices immediately, or to be alert to people's needs, or to perceive right away the risks to be taken.

Thus we are no longer as deaf, blind, or lazy when faced with God's calls. Like Isaiah, some of us hear the Lord saying, "Make justice your aim ... hear the orphan's plea, defend the widow." Like Christ, others see the crowds "lying prostrate from exhaustion." Like the Apostles, others feel the force of Jesus' invitation, "the hour is on us .... Get up! Let us be on our way!" (Is 1: 10; Mt 9: 36; 26: 45–46) Having become more sensitive, our heart is more easily touched when God speaks through events, confirming our specific vocation, reminding us of our personal "mission."

—— I remember a friend of mine, who had made several directed retreats, saying to me, "It does not take too long now for me to see my usual game. Recently, while giving a talk, in the twinkle of an eye, I caught myself playing 'The

Queen.' I was looking for my listeners' admiration. Immediately, I gave back to the group the opportunity to express their reactions, remembering God's call to me, 'Be a servant.' "

MANAGEMENT

As our awareness and our sensitivity about who we are (our name) and how we are called to act (our mission) grow clearer, our capacity to manage our life grows more effective as well. That is, we see more clearly what we can and cannot do, and how to live with that. We size up our strengths and our talents as well as our weaknesses and shortcomings. And we become more capable of making decisions that take account of the demands of the situation, but in a way that is true to ourselves. We become smarter managers of our life. Even when we must act quickly, our response will be more accurate because our practice of discernment has trained our reflexes to choose Life and not Death with a deepening certainty.

We are like bridge players: we have examined our hand, evaluated the length and strength of our trumps, and recognized where we are short-suited. And experience has shown us how to play our cards. Whether the situation calls for a show of strength or for biding our time, for acting promptly or waiting patiently, we have become "card sharks"!

—— A friend of mine, an ordained minister, had to confront her bishop. She opened their meeting by saying, "Even though I have a problem dealing with authority, I am going to try to express myself openly to you …. I know and believe that we are all brothers and sisters before God."

Our way of managing our life is our own answer to the call of a specific God. It is, of course, the One God who passionately desires the happiness of all human beings and the world's accomplishment through them. But in this moment it is a God who wants that through the fulfillment of our particular being and witness, and who knows and accepts our peculiar measurements. It is the God who calls and deals with each one of us "by name." (Is 43: 1) So, we are invited to take one more step ahead toward Agape in a very personal way, with the Spirit's help. God is no longer God only, but *our* God.

Therefore, sure of God's personal companionship with us, we can journey without fear, sure that we will overcome any obstacle, as did David going to battle with Goliath. (1 Sm 17: 45–47) And, for instance, if life becomes a way to Golgotha, we know that the Crucified One is going to walk with us, that our cross will be tailored to our size. (1 Co 10: 13)

Practicing discernment has helped us to see and experience with more clarity God's escort, to manage more consciously such company, to choose more personally to stay on the path of the One who is Agape. More and more all of our energy is liberated for whatever we may undertake. We say, with Paul, "I can do everything in the One who makes me strong." (Ph 4: 13; Mk 9: 23)

Now, we can act for we have everything necessary: we are "richly endowed" with knowledge, tools, and our portion of God's passionate love. (1 Co 1: 4–9) We can act more freely because we have been more fully liberated from what was enslaving us in the past. Therefore we have more capacity to take our lives into our own hands in a more conscious and responsible way: we are more able to manage our existence. It is up to us to put into action what we have discovered and decided and to go and work — as faithful servants put in charge and saying with Jesus, "My Father goes on working, and so do I." (Jn 5: 17)

QUESTIONS

INNER FREEDOM (INDIFFERENCE)

—— In my most recent decisions, where did I lack inner freedom?

—— In my current discernment, what am I clinging to? What is holding me captive?

—— What means have I used to sift through all the things I hang on to in order to find what is most fundamental in terms of my essential values and my religious faith?

—— In what sector of my life is the Lord calling me to greater inner freedom? Concerning what? Concerning whom?

—— What are the signs that are showing me whether I am growing more or less indifferent?

—— What means am I using to maintain my inner freedom all along the way in my current discernment? Who usually is my "Devil's Advocate"?

INCARNATION

—— In my most recent decisions, was I a "dreamer" forgetting who I *really* was, who people *really* were, what events *really* were like? What were the consequences of such a lack of realism?

—— In my current discernment, how am I going to take into account my talents and my limitations, people's qualities and shortcomings, the real dimensions of the events? What method will I use to make a serious analysis of the situation? Which experts am I going to consult? How can I take "one more step ahead" on that direction right now?

TO GIVE, TO BE GIVEN UP

—— In my most recent decisions, what did I refuse to give? How did I refuse to be given up to others?

—— In my current discernment, where do I see an invitation to give myself, to be given up? What is the "one more step ahead" I can afford?

UNIVERSALITY

—— In my most recent decisions, which part of myself have I usually ignored, denied? What were the consequences? Which people, which areas of my environment have I overlooked? Where was I too narrow-minded?

—— In my current discernment, what am I going to do in order to invest the whole of myself, in order to take into consideration more people, more areas of my environment than before? Where do I see "one more step ahead" in those directions?

COMMUNION

—— In my most recent decisions, did I see myself internally divided, torn apart — if so, between what extremes? In decisions I have made where I had to take into account opposing points of view, how did this invitation to openness affect me and my decision? How did I reconcile differences? Who have I never forgiven? Who can I never forgive?

FIFTH CRITERION

—— In my most recent decisions which criterion have I usually neglected or rejected? How am I going to take it into consideration in my current discernment?

LISTENING TO MY HEART

—— Do I remember experiencing different levels of emotions in my life? What were the physical signs and symptoms that told me I was affected at a very deep level? How did this change my usual behavior? Was I able to listen to my deepest feelings? Could I call them by name? When have I experienced "enlivening" feelings? "stifling" feelings? Why?

—— In my current discernment am I taking the time to let both alternatives sink in? Do I retreat to allow myself to listen to the echoes of my heart? What do I hear? How do I interpret these echoes? Which alternative suggested by my intellect gives me "enlivening" feelings and which one gives me "stifling" feelings?

REFINING THE DISCERNMENT

—— Do I remember which decision I made that was hard, in terms of feelings, but eventually turned out well for me? Can I pinpoint now just why it was hard, and why eventually it was beneficial? What kind of Passover, or Exodus, did I experience?

—— Do I remember any decision I made where I felt good at the beginning but the whole thing turned out to be a catastrophe? In what way did I contribute to the catastrophe? Can I trace the deviations of trajectory that took place? Can I remember the steps of the deterioration of my feelings?

—— Do I know now the sectors of my life where such deviations usually take place and can I recognize the pattern of such deviations? What signals given by my head and my heart must I take into account in order to avoid the same mistakes in those sectors?

PART THREE

Discernment by a Group of People

The preceding chapters have explained a method of discernment as it is practiced by an individual who is making a personal decision. This section will deal with two instances in which people interact in a group in order to discern. The first case occurs when an individual asks the members of the group to help him or her discern; the second situation concerns a group collaborating in some activity, and needing to come to a common decision about that activity.

CHAPTER

1

Others Help
Me to Discern

People frequently ask their friends for help when they are making a decision. It is true that others may play a very important and helpful role in our discernment, but their intervention may be also damaging. It is good to minimize the risks of the role played either by the friend or the group and to increase the likelihood of fruitful results when we do ask for help. Here is a way to systematize what we may have been doing all along, perhaps without a specific method.

Any serious dialogue with someone already entails an element of discernment, since expressing to another person what lies within us always clarifies what is in our minds and helps us to detect and identify the feelings of our hearts. The reaction of the other person gives us information about ourselves and, often, about other aspects of the issues we are considering. This kind of help is available as soon as we go to anyone for advice and, of course, we can get especially valuable assistance if the person is wise. But sometimes we may need even more than this. So, we go to people who have a certain expertise in the field, and when it is a question of discernment, we consult those who are qualified in spiritual matters. We can also refine our method of working with them.

It is quite possible if we are members of a group to enlist its help in our discernment. I would like to present a summa-

ry of a method practiced with good results by a group of believers of which I was a member. Of course, the effectiveness
of this method of discernment depends on the capacity of
each member of the group to make a personal discernment.
The better each member knows how to recognize the presence
of the Spirit of Agape in his or her own life, the more effectively the group will be able to serve the one who asks for
help. Even though Jesus said, "I tell you solemnly ... if two of
you on earth agree to ask anything at all, it will be granted to
you by my Father in heaven. For where two or three meet in
my name, I shall be there with them," we must remember that
the perception of his presence depends on our personal ability to discern it. (Mt 18: 19–20)

Describing and Listening

When someone asks a group for help, the members of the
group have to know, as clearly as possible, what the subject of
the discernment is. Without a minimum of information and
details, how can the group adequately grasp the question, the
problem in its frame, and its possible consequences? So, the
one involved in the situation must begin by describing what it
is all about.

It is very often a good idea for the person asking assistance
to prepare a written account of the main aspects of the search
and give it to the group in advance. The group needs to guarantee that the freedom of intimacy will be fostered, and priva-
cy preserved by a strong sense of confidentiality. It is helpful,
for instance, to specify the context out of which the question
has arisen. A historical description will include the length of
time, growth, evolution, modifications in the process, and the
stages experienced by the person asking for help. In fact,
through that work of *the intellect,* the group has already played
a part in allowing the problem to be clarified.

—— For example, a friend of mine explained the main steps of
    his emotional and spiritual history to our group. Then he

summarized the whole, "I joined the paratroopers and stayed with them for a couple of years in order to become courageous. Someday I realized it was deeper than courage — it was a question of self-esteem and guilt. I am living in fear and shame." It was quite clear, and we were able to understand who and where he was at this stage of his discernment.

But the intellectual description is never sufficient in itself. It is essential for the members of the group to have some idea of the feelings of *the heart* of the one looking for help, the attraction and the desire, the fear and hesitation, the peace and joy experienced, with regard to the subject of the discernment. To know the person's feelings allows the group to become aware of exactly what has been affecting the personal sensitivity of the one they want to help. My friend's words above are strong enough to show that.

At least this much candor is the responsibility of the seeker when he or she enters into dialogue with the group. But asking for help also requires another specific attitude: it is necessary for us to be ready to allow what is said by others to enter into our own point of view and to alter our original thoughts. Openness is not always easy, but here it is indispensable. I still remember how uneasy we felt as group members each time a certain man came to us for help. He had already made up his mind, a fact we had verified several times before. We never knew why he came to us. Was he only looking for our approval? Was he trying to please us by a semblance of openness? Did he want to be able to tell outsiders that his decision was backed by the group? Or was there something lacking in the way the group listened? — because the group had its role to play.

The primary responsibility of the people who make up the group is to listen and to question in a particular way. Above all, it is essential for them to realize that this man or woman is trying to communicate something that is difficult to articulate, because it has to do with the relationship between him or her — as a human being — and God. It is the expression of a mystery.

Grasping in our own mind and heart our companionship and adventure with the Lord is already more than a challenge. How much greater the difficulty of describing and explaining that to others. In the group I belonged to, some sharings had the effect of a revelation: standing beyond the words spoken with conscious openness, honesty, and simplicity was the "pillar of cloud," both shining and obscure, that led the Hebrews. (Ex 13: 21) We who listened were in awe as were the ones who watched Moses going into the meeting Tent. (Ex 33: 7–10)

When we choose to share such an intimate side of our lives, we often feel as if we are stripping ourselves of our clothing and exposing our nakedness before others. It is a beautiful demonstration of courage and confidence but, unless we are exhibitionists, it is also an enormous risk for our vulnerability. The listening group must be extremely respectful and questioning must be done with extreme delicacy. We cannot insist enough on this because needless exhibitionism and stripping, probing and peeling have been the plague of some groups who were acting in the name of the myth of transparency. The awareness of what is at stake when someone reveals himself or herself does not totally remove the risk. But it will help everyone to maintain a healthy reserve that will prevent one from becoming a voyeur or rapist. It should be evident that it may be necessary for the one asking for help to complete the process of discernment by a dialogue with a spiritual "accompanist" with whom more can be unveiled than can be expressed in a group.

We have to proceed step by step in the undertaking we are describing, progressively taming one another. As a matter of fact, I have noticed that the more the group practices this process, the less inquisitive the members become and the more deeply respectful and discreet they grow. Fears disappear even though some taboos may persist. We are no longer defendants before judges or torturers, but sisters and brothers before the mystery of God, each one of us at the entrance of our tent looking toward the place where the Lord talks "mouth to mouth" to the faithful one who asks for help. (Ex 33: 9–11)

REFLECTING AND PRAYING

Once the one asking for help has described the situation, it is very good for the members of the group to reflect and pray on the issues given them. Reflection cannot be separated from praying if we really look at our companion as a unique son or daughter of the Father of Jesus, who wants to understand and faithfully answer a call of love. So, each member of the group takes into account what is now known about their friend's capacities and limitations, talents and weaknesses, temptations and failures. With all of that information before them in an atmosphere of prayer, each one tries to answer the question, "In the light of the best that I wish for my companion, what would be possible for him or her right now?" Using the criteria given earlier in this book, for instance, each person attempts to discern what could be the "one more step ahead" that might be the call from the Spirit of Life and Love.

This kind of work is the love in action of all the partners. It is their love for the Father of Jesus — Father of us all, for their brother and sister, for all the people who will be touched by the decision to come. It is also God's love in action through them, through their own love, especially right now for this beloved one who is discerning. Therefore, they must look at their friend with love and mercy as the Lord does.

Helping someone to discern may seem like a duty — something we do *for the other*, but it is also a grace *for us*. God dares to use us as instruments for helping one of Jesus' brothers or sisters say "yes." We have the inestimable privilege to stand in front of the Holy of Holies where the Lord is sealing a new phase of the Covenant with a chosen one. (Ex 33) We are called to be careful lest we intrude!

Sometimes the sense of awe before a mystery becomes so powerful that prayer wells up in the group. Once, listening to one of our companions explaining his desire to become an ordained minister, we all became perceptibly engulfed in a deeper and deeper silence. When one of the group recommended that we start to pray, most of us were astonished that he felt he needed to recommend setting out toward the One who had already overtaken us.

We cannot help being invited to pray if we are aware of what is going on in this kind of encounter. The kind of dialogue we are talking about is not a job interview, even though it requires the same kind of serious intent as any honest business. It is not group psychotherapy, even though the work we do there is improved by our consciousness of the interplay of the psychological dynamics involved and by our ability to handle them. It is not merely a session of group dynamics, even though it is certainly appropriate to use effective group techniques and tools as well as the skills of a group facilitator.

This experience of collective discernment is something more awesome. As a group we prepare the way for a brother or sister to embark on a new stage in the great adventure with the Lord God. We help an Abraham go forth to a new land, we assist another Moses in a new Exodus, we help another Esther to go to her king. Often the experience sends us back to our own journey and invites us "to walk humbly" with our companion, "with our God." (Mi 6: 8)

"YOUR POINT OF VIEW BUT MY OWN RESPONSIBILITY"

After a period of *time*, the members of the group gather together again. The length of the period of separation depends on many factors. It depends on the relative importance of this decision in the person's life, for example, or the time limit for making a choice, or whether or not there is information to be gathered or experience to be gained about certain aspects of the issue.

When we are together again, we each express our opinions, suggestions, and reactions very freely but always recalling that we are expressing our own points of view. We are not telling people what to do! It may be helpful to begin each statement with a formula such as, "It seems to me that ...." In this way the pros and cons seen by each member are put forward. The seeker may want to ask for more explanations or the rationale behind certain opinions. A type of discussion may take place among the members of the group.

The members speak freely because they realize that this is not, in fact, their own decision; the beneficiary is free also, understanding that he or she listens to ideas expressed only as opinions. The one who needs to discern listens to the whole presentation using the kind of sensitivity we have described earlier, that is, trying to hear the echoes produced in the heart by all that is said. Sometimes it may be necessary for the person to replay the entire dialogue at another time in order to discern quietly what awakens the Spirit of Life and Love or the power of Death within. In any case, at the end of the meeting, this is the time for the one asking for help on the journey to say, "Thank you for your input. Now, I must go back to myself and God with all that you have given me and assume responsibility for my own decision."

Even though I am nurtured and enlightened by my companions, I must make my own discernment and choice. *Alone.* Solitude is the price of freedom, and freedom to choose is the basis of human dignity. Yet, at this point, even if I am alone, I am not isolated and, although my decision is really mine, it is not arbitrary because it is, somehow ours also. My friends have walked with me as far as they could go. Someone once said to me, "Choosing community life, I thought that decisions would be easier; in fact, thanks to my respectful companions, I was invited to assume responsibility for myself at deeper and deeper levels. It was awful to be treated not as a baby, but rather as an adult by people who did not act as mothers, fathers, guardians or judges, but as my true brothers and sisters ... it was awful but beautiful. I felt my dignity."

If I am one of the group members I must accept the decision of our friend nonjudgmentally, respecting the freedom of this man or woman facing God's call. I may agree or disagree, it does not matter. What I said, in fact, has become a part of the choice.

Suppose that my friend refuses the inspiration of the Spirit, whether manifested through the group or within himself or herself. I must remember everyone's right to be weak, to be a sinner, as well as each one's right to be treated with compassion, to be forgiven. After all, that's the way the Lord deals with all of us, including myself. Our societies, our churches, all of us have much to learn about freedom and mercy. "If there is one of you who has not sinned, let him be the first to throw a stone at her," said Jesus. (Jn 8: 7)

And, of course, if my friend chooses to say "yes" to God, I will rejoice.

GIVING THANKS

Throughout the entire process we all have many reasons to be thankful. At the beginning someone said to us, "Please, help me to discern," and through this prayer uttered by our companion we have heard God begging us, "Please, help my beloved listen to me." All along the way our partner has felt the constant concern and love of the Spirit through our human flesh as respectful, caring brothers and sisters — like a new incarnation of God's love in humankind. At the end of the encounter we recognize in the thanks expressed to us by the one who discerns God's own gratitude and joy for what we have done. Similarly, when we say, "Thank you, for you have trusted us as servants of the Spirit for you," our partner will hear a grateful God saying, "I thank you for believing in my presence in your brothers and sisters, my sons and daughters."

We have all become signs for one another, sacraments of God's Love. We have been chosen to prepare the way of the Lord. (Lk 17: 10; 1: 76) When we are drawn into the experience of Mary and Elizabeth we can only exult and give thanks, for God has done great things for and through us. (Lk 1: 39–55)

CHAPTER
2

We Want to Discern for a Common Decision

L et us consider the members of a group needing to come to a common decision. Before describing the method by which we can do this, let us clarify some prerequisite conditions.

PRELIMINARY CONSIDERATIONS

The following remarks are preliminary in the sense that ignoring them affects and may damage any attempt to practice communal discernment.

DON'T BE NAIVE, IT'S A FIGHT
TO THE FINISH

As far as I know, it is difficult in the Christian tradition to find a set of directives for a systematic method of discernment that can be used by a group. The reason for the unavailability of an outline of how to proceed may be that, when we undertake the process of such a discernment, we are confronted with a very real obstacle. It is better for us to face this difficulty right from the start.

God is *the* unique Being; each one of us is a unique human being; therefore, the relationship between the Lord and each human being cannot be duplicated. At the deepest level of discernment, what happens between God and me cannot happen the same way as between God and someone else. So, how can we believe that it is possible for several people to become unanimous at the deepest level of their being in a common decision? History is full of internal divisions among the members of a group as far as the tower of Babel. (Gn 11) According to the Acts of the Apostles and Paul's letters, even the oneness of the early Church, so clearly and wonderfully experienced on Pentecost (however, each disciple spoke in a different language), did not last very long. (Acts 2) Admitting then that we cannot really find a systematic method of discernment that will guarantee group unanimity at the deepest level, the best we can do is to propose some ways of approaching a difficult task, some tactics for reaching what approximates a real, deep common decision. Our acknowledgment of the basic underlying difficulty prepares us to deal with two potentially troublesome outcomes when we use the process that will be described.

First, we will not be surprised if discerning together is difficult and brings forth tensions and conflicts. This is normal and cannot be otherwise, and we do not have to be afraid of this. As it is implied in any other common-union, communion, some separations have to be overcome between the partners. Therefore, a kind of labor, which can be painful, must be done.

Second, we will be wary of jumping to unwarranted conclusions when, as members of a group, we appear to be too easily unanimous about something important. What might have we overlooked? Have the members of the group been tired or lazy? Have we not felt free enough to express ourselves or have we been manipulated? Were we not well enough informed or were we too "obedient"? Except in urgent cases, it would be better to take *time* to check that out right from the beginning. It took painful weeks and sharp conflicts for the delegates who wrote the Constitution of the United States, for example, but who would regret the labor needed to give birth to democracy?

DO WE HAVE THE SAME STARTING POINT?

When a group desires to undertake a communal discernment in order to reach a common decision, there is already something that links its members together. This common bond may be a philosophy, a creed, a vision, an interest, a goal, or a project that is accepted or shared by all. If we continue to use the case of the writing of the Constitution as an example, we recognize quickly how Abraham Lincoln viewed the common aim of most of its authors: to create "a new nation, conceived in liberty, and dedicated to the proposition that all men are created equal."

In many cases the goals of a group are presumed to be common and taken for granted. We say for example, "Because we believe in the same God or values, for the good of the family, or for the sake of the business, let's do this or that …." But what is really behind the words we use? A lack of clarity about the goal from the beginning may be the cause of the problems that arise once the "rocket is launched." Often we speak of our goal with the same words, but it is necessary to express and explain as much as possible what lies behind them in our mind. Otherwise the unacknowledged differences that exist among us may lead us to betray one another later. In the example of the formation of the Union of the States of America it would be enlightening to compare what we, today, understand as the meaning of the words, "We, the people …." It is probably not exactly what the drafters, *white men,* had in mind. In the initial stages of the development of Christianity, the local Churches (Jerusalem, Antioch, Ephesus, Smyrna, Pergamum, etc.) would disclose to each other the Creed they professed in order to be sure that they really shared the same faith. In Acts 19, for example, we can see that the word *baptism* did not mean the same thing for Paul as it did for the disciples of John the Baptist.

Of course, life gives us surprises every day, and we can never predict with certainty what tomorrow will bring, but it still depends on us to check out from the beginning whether we really have *a common starting point.* No common discernment is possible or fruitful for a group without the verification, and the certainty, that all its members share the same aiming at the deepest level.

As members of a group we must reflect on and talk about our fundamental agreement. A deep and honest communication is needed here, stemming from the desires and convictions that each one carries within. It's a sharing of our values, our faith, absolutely necessary when an important decision has to be made. What is essential remains, too often, implicit among us. But such a deep sharing demands that we sustain (or create) the kind of habitual climate of exchange that allows and invites this kind of self-disclosure.

What do we mean, for example, when we say "God"? Is my God a God of compassion or a judge? What is a "Christian," for me? A person called to serve or someone who owns the truth? Is nonviolence in my life a means of creating political pressure or a stance that I want to adopt personally? Is the Equal Rights Amendment an opportunity to attack men or a question of justice for all? We may guess that the choices we make will be the outcome of the way we think. That is why when we try to discern as a group for an important common decision, we must ask ourselves and each other with respect and care, "What do you mean?"

ONE FINAL CONDITION

Here we meet a sine qua non condition. According to what was said above in this book, we are only able to articulate our faith and our goals if we have been able to clarify them for ourselves: in other words if we have usually been capable of personal discernment. As a matter of fact, when I question myself or I am questioned by others about what I find essential when I say, "God, Christian, nonviolence, Equal Rights Amendment," it is assumed that I will express what is fundamental *for me,* for *my head and my heart* in the notions we mentioned.

A communal discernment deserves to be qualified as discernment only if each member of the group has acquired through practice the capacity of discerning personally. If that condition is not fulfilled, a group can still make decisions but it would be better not to call the process used discernment. In that case, people do what they can but they cannot expect to get the guarantees given by discernment. If we are aware of this, then we will not be disturbed about the imperfections in the attempts we make together, nor disappointed with the results, because we will recognize the limitations of a process that is not really discernment. In fact, in some cases people have been abused by leaders or members of a group in which they experienced a dangerous and damaging group dynamic, a so-called discernment of God's will.

It's when people have determined what they all agree on that they can go further. Undertaking the clarification I have described answers the question, "Where do we all come from and where do we all want to go?" It is like pinpointing on a map where we are right now and deciding if we all want to go to the same place. Only after checking that out can we look at the roads we will take for our shared journey.

THERE ARE ALWAYS MANY WAYS AND MEANS

The image of the map immediately reminds us that several roads may exist to get to the same place. When we travel together, one of us who values high speed and efficient use of fuel may recommend the freeway; someone else who loves riding along gazing at the scenery will prefer the meandering route through the mountains; another companion, a problem solver by nature, would like to show us her favorite shortcut by the back roads. Agreement on the starting point and the destination does not necessarily imply agreement about the route to follow.

Therefore it is not surprising if, once we have an initial agreement, we face another wave of conflicts when it comes time to choose the ways and means to reach the goal.

Why would we expect to be different from Paul and Barnabas, so "unanimous" in their sense of mission to the Gentiles, who disagreed, and even separated, because of a nonessential problem? (Acts 15: 36–40) It is obvious that Jesus, James, and John had different ways and means in mind for treating the inhospitable Samaritans. (Lk 9: 51–56) The fact is that such differences may not be a catastrophe at all: may God be blessed that, in most cases, several solutions exist ... for our freedom (any dictatorship is characterized by "one way").

Diversity is enriching for the group and may reveal solutions that have been forgotten by most of the members: "Why not fly instead of drive?" A multiplicity of means multiplies approaches and concrete realizations. Instead of one team for a mission, Paul and Barnabas, the early Church ended with two: Paul and Silas, Barnabas and Mark. Serving the poor can be lived out by dwelling in a slum, by exerting an influence on politicians or the media, by creating unions in areas where laborers are exploited, by revealing "The Other America" in the classroom .... The options are as limited as our creativity and our freedom within our historical circumstances.

The group proposes all possible solutions to the problem by using methods such as brainstorming, small group discussions in dyads, triads, etc. However, when we have finished proposing all of the possible solutions, we will need to analyze them. It might be that some of the solutions are in contradiction with the values or faith of the group or the desired goal, or both. If Jesus reprimanded James and John, it was because calling down fire from heaven to destroy the Samaritans was a means of resolving a problem obviously not in keeping with Agape. (Lk 9: 54)

SCREENING WITH INDIFFERENCE

Analyzing all the means suggested by the group is screening them. Together the partners look at the pros and cons for each one of them and keep only the means that fit the common purpose. The essential tool that everyone needs at this stage is the honesty of indifference.

As one of the group, if I am able to remain indifferent, I can accept and even back a solution proposed by someone else, for instance, without trying to refuse it surreptitiously because I do not like it. Similarly, indifference permits me to see the proposal I have submitted eventually rejected by others without becoming furious or destroyed.

When we are all indifferent, our screening is always led by the values, faith, and goal, we *all prefer*. Suppose a group of us is traveling together to attend an important business meeting that requires our being on time. Then enjoying the landscape cannot be an important consideration. We need to find the most direct way. So, we might decide to take the highway and not the route through the mountains or the back roads, for example.

It's our intellect that is at work here, keeping in mind the values, the faith we all share. But the business of our head will be more certain as long as we do everything to maintain ourselves in indifference, free in our heart, in the way described in the chapters on individual discernment. Indifference preserves us from the narrowness of our own ideas, our particular interests and our conscious or subconscious desires. We can see how necessary it is for each member of the group to be experienced in individual discernment.

When the process is working well, when I am indifferent, and the others are as well, I no longer try to win my point for my own satisfaction. I would rather submit myself to the common goal that our common values, our common faith defined. Each "I" serves the "We," the impetus for our being one. As a Christian involved in a communal discernment, each person serves Someone Else, the same Spirit of God believed in by all, Agape whose witnesses they all together want to be. At this stage of the process the members of the group are already behaving in a way that proclaims, "The Holy Spirit *and* ourselves …" because each one uses his or her talents "for the common good." (Acts 15: 28; 1 Co 12: 7) It is only by indifference that the means suggested by the members of the group are purified by the Spirit from selfish motivations.

A SPECIAL WAY OF LISTENING TO EACH OTHER

When the suggestions that have been made are discussed by the members of the group, a specific kind of listening must take place in order to make this stage of the process a part of discernment. It is not simply a question of hearing and discussing information as we do in a conversation that takes place outside this context. Here, if we take Christians as an example, the partners must use their spiritual sensitivity if they really want to discern the Spirit of Agape. Yes through, but also behind, the information and the opinions offered by each member, they have to listen to each other and debate according to the values of the Spirit found in the Scriptures, and first of all, in the words and behavior of Jesus.

Mobilizing all their spiritual sensitivity to Christ's message, they seek to grasp *the evangelical values and the elements of the Good News* that are present in someone's remarks and that give worth and weight to them. That special way of listening to each other may be sensitive to a concern for the poorest ones, for example, or to communion among people, to a sense of justice or to merciful forgiveness … let us say, sensitive to what is in harmony with Agape, as we have said in the chapter *How to Work with My Head.* Using the example of our travelers who needed to choose the appropriate way of arriving at their destination, maybe they would have rejected the proposal to travel by plane as not in keeping with their preference for evangelical poverty.

Here is one of the best examples that I have seen. A new area was being developed in our city. Since this center was foreseen as an economic and administrative hub, the layout included many bank headquarters as well as offices for the city and the regional government. Many religious groups were inclined to favor the presence of the Churches in that section. During a meeting to discuss a proposal to settle some religious communities in the area, an urban planner, informed about the city's future, talked about the projected space saying, "It will be the nerve center of the city and of the region as well: the center of *power*. I hope the Churches will not rush there. If they do, it will signify that they always seek to be where the power is." That reflection hit home for all of us. We were reminded of all the refusals of Jesus to compromise with money and power. (Mt 6: 24; Lk 22: 24–27; etc.)

We can understand now why I emphasized earlier the necessity for all the associates in this work to identify as clearly as possible their common values, faith, and goal at the beginning of their discernment: all along the process each person has to keep going back, unceasingly, to those roots of the unanimity of the group.

PRAYER

Indifference and listening to "the Spirit's words to the Churches," as John says, are essential conditions for discernment for a Christian group. (Rv 2) The equivalent is true for groups of nonbelievers or believers who must try to be free within themselves in order to hear the spirit of their value system or their religious tradition.

Staying with the instance of a Christian group, all along the discernment process *prayer* is absolutely necessary. The kind of inner freedom we are talking about, indifference, is not given by "flesh and blood." It is a gift of the Spirit of Christ. This one said, " ... if the Son makes you free, you will be free indeed." (Mt 16: 17; Jn 8: 36) Only God can free a sinner from selfishness. So, it is a grace that must be asked for. All together as a group and each one separately, the members are invited to pray for such a gift.

The same necessity exists for the special way of listening to each other. If John in the Book of Revelation proclaims seven times the same invitation cited above, it is only because he repeats what Jesus said, "If anyone has ears to hear, let him listen!" (Mt 11: 15; 13: 9, 43) That must be repeated often, for this kind of hearing is not spontaneous for us. The Lord cured a deaf-mute. In this miracle all the Churches have always seen the physical description of the grace of becoming able to hear God's Word. (Mk 7: 31–37) Here also we are talking about a grace that must be asked for.

Indeed, it is a grace because, as human beings, we cannot take for granted that we are immediately in tune with Agape. It may even be more difficult in a group where the proximity of others and the debate with them can amplify the unconscious vulnerability of each person who gets caught up in the dynamics of the group. At a deeper level, only the grace of God can show up "the foolishness of human wisdom," which so attracts us all; God only can make the faithful able to accept "nothing but Jesus Christ and him crucified"— the Agape we are all called to let enter our lives. (1 Co 1: 21; 2: 2)

THE MOMENT OF DECISION

The final stage of the process of communal discernment is similar to the same stage in this process for an individual. Having screened the proposed solutions, the group seeks and finds the means most suitable for the realization of the initial project. Sometimes several means may be discovered and especially when the same goal is pursued by partners who are specialists in diverse fields (remember, for example, that we mentioned different ways of serving the poor).

There are many examples of groups who have shared a common goal coming to a common decision: the Constitutional Convention of the early United States finally agreed to found an independent nation with a democratic form of government; Henry Ford, Sr., and his staff decided to pay their employees high salaries for selling the cars that the company manufactured; the U. S. government, desiring to rebuild Western Europe as a political ally and a commercial partner after World War II, created the Marshall Plan. And the twelve Apostles, after a period of discernment, decided not to force Pagans entering the Church to follow all the Jewish rites. (Acts 15)

Interestingly, in Acts 15, we find words that express the feelings of those Christians. Before the decision of the Twelve, they were "upset." When they got word of the decision made in Jerusalem, they were in "great delight." Is it surprising to read that? At the end of the narrative that relates another famous discernment, one made by Ignatius of Loyola and his first nine companions in 1539 when they founded the Society of Jesus, we read, "That final day all our business was complete and terminated in a spirit of gladness and harmony." No surprise, for usually, as we said of individual discernment, when the process has worked very well, the associates enjoy "enlivening" feelings. Why? Certainly we experience peace and joy whenever we reach an agreement with our partners, and the more important the decision, the deeper the feelings. But when the decision is the outcome of discernment, the peace and joy experienced are the result of a unanimity not founded on compromise but in communion.

Christians would say that being, at last, one in the Spirit of Jesus they savor not the world's peace but the one given by the Lord. (Jn 14: 27) For he promised, "You will live in my love if you keep my commandments, even as I have kept my Father's commandments and live in his love. All this I tell you that my joy may be yours and your joy may be complete." (Jn 15: 10–11) When they keep the commandment of Agape from the beginning to the end of their discernment, they enjoy within themselves, individually, and all together as a group, the fulfillment of the prayer of Jesus, "May they be one ...." (Jn 17: 21)

I have cited the discernment of Ignatius and his companions here for several reasons. One is that, as far as I know, it is the only written report available of a discernment made by a group of Christians all trained in individual discernment. Another reason is that everything said so far in the chapter *We Want to Discern for a Common Decision,* has been extracted from the experience described in that text. A third reason is that the second part of that account leads us further to the point I am about to explain.

REFINING THE DISCERNMENT

In brief, this is what happened to those first Jesuits. In 1534, at Montmartre near Paris, the initial seven vowed themselves to Jesus' service and went out, two by two, to work in Europe. In 1539, back together with three new friends, they wanted to decide whether they were called to remain bound to one another. After an initial discernment, they agreed (what we have said so far in the chapter *We Want to Discern for a Common Decision,* came from that first step of their discernment). But that decision created a further question. They wondered if they wanted to stay together as a religious order. The new question implied the problem of making a vow of obedience to one of the group. So, they began another discernment, refining the tools they had used for the first one.

In this situation, the new question was one that touched the very deepest level of each companion's being: his individual freedom. At the same time it raised the greatest temptation, the lust for power. When the members of a group perceive that they are facing a very serious decision, one that has to do with the core of human life, they would do better to refine their discernment, by perfecting the tools we have already described and by adding some new ones.

The kind of grave circumstance I am referring to arises, for example, when the associates risk their physical lives in making a certain choice; when political pressure would coerce them to

compromise their art; or if they have to risk losing their reputation to make an ethical decision; or if they should have to
confront religious persecution. At the same time the question
of having one more child in a large family is a grave enough
case for a serious discernment for a couple, as is whether to
adopt a child. And it does not hurt to improve our discernment
in lighter matters as well.

MORE WATCHFUL IN PRAYER

In situations like these, believers will find it wise and helpful to do what those Jesuit companions did. They prayed more.
It means for the members of a group to try to be more alert to
what is happening in prayer, and not simply to accumulate
prayers — and that, at least for three reasons.

First, the associates must ask God to increase their *indifference* in order to remove from them, as much as possible, the influence of their destructive subconscious motivations. It would
certainly be damaging to adopt a child out of a desire to acquire
supplemental income, for example.

Second, it is necessary to pray for *light*. In such a plight,
people need the greatest possible certainty because a mistake
would be too costly. It is a catastrophe for the couple, the family, and the child in the case of a misguided adoption. It is a
useless ordeal if losing their reputation destroys what a group
might accomplish in the future.

Third, praying will give *strength* in order to be able to deal
with the results of the common decision. Without strength the
sacrifice of one's art might become an unbearable self-destruc-
tion; the confrontation with persecution might lead to aposta-
sy, the appalling consequence of an unrefined discernment.

REFLECTION AND SOLITUDE

"Go into your room by yourself, shut the door ...." (Mt 6:
6) In addition to prayer, the partners used another tool:

None of the companions would communicate with
any other about the matter at issue or inquire about his

reasoning on it. The point of this preparation was to prevent anyone from being persuaded by another and, therefore, biased more toward obedience. This way each would desire as more advantageous only what derived from his own prayer and meditation.

Even though they had been friends for years, they would not permit themselves to discuss the question under consideration with one another before their personal discernment was terminated. When the question that is before the group concerns each individual at the core of himself or herself, then it is better to avoid any external influence. Absolute priority must be given to solitude in order to be sure that each associate will be reflecting (and praying) alone and will be enlightened by his or her own personal convictions and by the indwelling Spirit.

A group can easily exert pressure on an individual, inhibiting his or her freedom: political intrigue and emotional blackmail are realities. So we need to observe firmly all possible precautions that this kind of pressure will not be operative when a serious decision has to be made: when each spouse considers the possibility of an adoption, for example, or when each of the partners in a common enterprise is facing grave danger. No one can stand in the place of another before the Lord. Today we find great value in sharing and this can be truly enriching for everybody. But we need to remember to go back to ourselves in silence and solitude and to take the *time* to check out what we will discover *by ourselves.* Some friends of mine, discerning about an adoption, arranged some time together to share their ideas and feelings about it, but they were careful to give each other several days between encounters in order to allow time for personal discernment.

DO WE NEED AN OUTSIDER?

As a means of looking at the question objectively and preserving the greatest possible inner liberty, each one of the companions of Ignatius was invited "to think of himself as a stranger" to the group and "one who would have no expectation of joining it." Then, from this perspective, each was asked "to speak his thought to the group about having or not having obedience." The purpose of this was to assure "thinking this way he would escape being carried away by his emotions more to one opinion and judgment."

This is a very difficult exercise, but it is a very effective device for preparing people to receive the grace of indifference. It is always helpful to try it. Each member is invited to ask himself or herself the question, "If I were a stranger, not belonging to the group and not involved in its problem, what would I say about the advantages and the disadvantages of each of the alternatives?" By inducing a kind of inner "split personality," it allows each one some distance from the emotional impact of the issue. The mind separates itself, as much as possible, from the power of the "guts" in order to reflect on the situation more objectively. This technique is actually more commonly used than we might think. We use it whenever we ask someone else, "If you were me, what would you say about my problem?" As a matter of fact, wouldn't it have been much easier for the ten companions to call in a real "outsider"? Why didn't they do that?

Why didn't they consult ministers, religious, or lay people? We cannot say exactly, but we may assume that one reason might have been to preserve their freedom. The majority of lay people interested in the organization and the problems of the churches at that time were kings and princes. We know what they did when they were allowed to interfere: quite often it was not for the best of Christianity. Another reason might have been that most of the companions had been educated at the Sorbonne in Paris. They must have been sufficiently armed intellectually to resolve by themselves the problem they faced. Finally, on a spiritual level, they had all been well-trained about personal discernment through *The Spiritual Exercises* of Ignatius.

I like to stress once more the absolute necessity of a personal capacity for individual discernment for each one of us when we are members of a group that needs to reach a common decision. This, remember, is the sine qua non. But today, a real outsider might well be invited to be a part of the communal process. Consultation with people outside the group is more and more unavoidable in our complex world where we can no longer claim to be competent in every field — as the Jesuit companions could do in their time. Experts may become, in our century, precious and necessary sources of information for our discernment. But we need an outsider whose competency and honesty are unquestionable.

A PARTICULAR WAY OF CONSIDERING
THE PROS AND CONS

When the companions had finished making their personal discernment, they informed each other of the results, simply and frankly. They did this in two steps. First, each one presented only his reasons *against* obedience, his cons. Then, days later each one presented his reasons *for* obedience, his pros. And they repeated the process until they came to a decision.

This might seem like a strange approach, but there are some well-founded reasons for following it (and I have verified what follows, in a group of friends). Above all, it promotes *unanimity*. For while they were presenting both the pros and cons, they were together as *one* in the process. They were either *all for it* or *all against it*. Partisan discussions and angry debates can be avoided by using this method and listening is certainly fostered. By contrast, when this person presents an argument and that one reacts immediately with an opposing view, they are easily pitted against each other as opponents, and they would tend to defend their own ideas without opening themselves to each other. This technique reduces the risk of that happening.

Perhaps, too, this device, starting with the cons, may permit a group to see, right away, any insuperable obstacle to carrying out the project. Arguments like these might be proposed, for example: "We cannot adopt a child because I have just lost my job. So we cannot even afford the legal fees involved in the adoption procedure." Or "We cannot go to that country. The political situation is in such turmoil that nothing is possible." Or "We cannot go back to that poor part of the world because of the physical health of my husband. He can no longer cope with the climate."

Finally, each member knows ahead of time that the others will all follow the same track — all against the proposal or all for it. Expecting no opposition from anyone, everyone feels freer to express openly, fearlessly, and without reserve whatever he or she has discovered personally.

Then, day after day, the companions weighed what they had said and heard in order to find "which alternative" appeared "more reasonable" (*The Spiritual Exercises*, 182), and, eventually, made their common decision — which was to found together a new religious order, the Society of Jesus:

> Our efforts lasted for almost three months, from the middle of Lent until the feast of John the Baptist. On that day, but not without long vigils, much prayer and labor of mind and body preceding deliberation and decision, all our business was complete and terminated in a spirit of gladness and harmony.*

Three months? We are back to the beginning of this book, when we started talking about the framework, *time*. Yes, it takes time. Haste has nothing to do with an authentic discernment.

---

* The whole narrative of this discernment can be found in an English translation by Jules J. Toner, S.J., in *Studies in the Spirituality of the Jesuits*, vol. VI, No. 4, June 1974, under the title, "The Deliberation That Started the Jesuits," a commentary on the *Deliberatio priorum patrorum*, with an historical introduction. For the address of the publishers, see Suggested Readings at the end of this book.

QUESTIONS

THE ONE SEEKING HELP

— How do I go about preparing the presentation of my problem? (e.g., Did I make an outline, list chronologically the significant events, bring any relevant documents?)

— To what degree am I open about revealing my feelings about what happened, without exhibitionism?

— How have I prepared myself to be ready to listen openly to any question or suggestion while remembering that I must stay free and responsible for the decision to come? (What was my reaction the last time I was offered a suggestion or was asked a question I did not like?)

THE GROUP MEMBERS

— How do I respect confidentiality?

— How do I demonstrate my attitude of respect for the one who is talking? (e.g., How do I ask questions? How do I make suggestions?)

— How do I show that I have understood the facts that have been reported and the feelings that have been expressed?

— Where, in my listening, have I made a space to consider the values of the person who is speaking, his or her stage in journeying with God?

— How seriously do I pray about the process?

— How will I respond if the decision made is one I do not like?

— Am I aware and grateful that it is a privilege and a grace to be asked to help someone else?

DISCERNING FOR A COMMON DECISION

— How often have we practiced individual discernment before facing a common decision?

— How do we deal with conflicting ideas, feelings, and personalities?

— How long do we need to verify whether we have the same starting point?

—— How often, in our deliberations, have we gone back to our common goal, values, and faith? our "vision" and "mission"?

—— What safeguards have we adopted to protect each individual's freedom? (from politics, intrigue, coalitions, etc.)

—— How often do we pray individually and together about the process?

—— What procedure do we follow when we select an outside expert?

—— How do we integrate what the expert offers into our common goal values, faith — "vision" and "mission"?

FOR ALL

—— What about the poor?

Final Reflections on Our Decisions

THE LAST TEST AND JUDGMENT

Jesus said to the people, "When you see a cloud rising in the West you say that rain is coming, and it does. And when the wind is from the South you say it will be hot, and it is. Hypocrites! You know how to interpret the face of the earth and the sky. How is it that you do not know how to interpret these times?" (Lk 12: 54–56) Could Jesus make the same reproach today? The fact that many Jews could not discern who he was, in spite of what they saw and heard and even though he stood before them in flesh and blood, shows that recognizing him was not as easy as we sometimes naively imagine.

Is it really any more difficult to discern the presence of his Spirit right now in our life? We have all experienced our blindness and deafness as spouses or as parents, as friends or as colleagues, and as citizens. That is why we must learn to discern more systematically if we want to be with the Lord of Love in the "flesh" of our family, social, economic, and political life. Discerning more methodically helps us to see the signs of the wind of the Spirit blowing, hear where the Spirit is whispering, discover where and how we are called to serve Agape. (Jn 3: 8; Rom 8: 26–27; 1 Kgs 19: 12–13)

"Seeing … hearing … serving": these words bring us to the *ultimate* verification of the value of our discernment and decision. If you are surprised to find a final test here at the end of

107

these pages, I invite you to go to Matthew's gospel and there you will find it similarly placed. In Matthew this standard is found at the end of Jesus' preaching and points to the end of time when we all face the *last* Judgment. (Mt 25: 31–46)

Jesus said, "For I was hungry and you gave me food. I was thirsty and you gave me drink. I was a stranger and you made me welcome, naked and you clothed me, sick and you visited me, in prison and you came to see me." And people asked, "Where, when did we see you in such a situation?" We know the answer well, "I assure you, as often as you did it for one of my least brothers, you did it for me." Matthew inserts the test just before Jesus' Passion. When the time came for him to be imprisoned and naked on the cross, to be one of the poorest crucified ones, the Apostles were not there. "Were you there, when they crucified my Lord?" asks the song … the Twelve had fled, denied, and betrayed. They failed the test.

Whether we discern individually or collectively in any circumstances, eventually we are tested in our decision by the way we see the poor, hear their cries, and serve them. *The poor have priority.*

There are people with no knowledge of a systematic method of discernment who have never passed the Lord by in their lives as the priest and the Levite did in the parable of the Good Samaritan. They are like the one who was "moved to pity" at the sight of his injured brother. (Lk 10: 25–37) In the movement of compassion, the melodies of Agape are sung together. And that is why this test is infallible.

When we take into account, for instance, the one who is suffering the most right now, we are *incarnate*. We *give* when we serve that poor one and we are *given up* when we allow the sorrow of this one to become the center of our attention. We take a step toward *universality* when we break out of our own circle to reach out to the one who is outcast, excluded, ignored, or marginalized. *Communion* lies at the very root of compassion: *cum-patire*, in Latin means to suffer-with someone. If we accept the assertion of Meister Eckhart, "Whatever God does, the first outburst is always compassion," then compassion in us is the surer sign of God's presence and action.

While it is true that there are some people so attuned to the Spirit of God, the Spirit of Compassion, that they seem to operate quite naturally out of Agape, who are we to assume that we are among them? Wouldn't it be better to be and live Agape with compassion for the poor *and at the same time* discern methodically? Let us hope that each one of us, and all of us together, may grow deeper in compassion through discernment so that we may become more and more able to say with John, to a world yearning for this Good News of Agape in our human flesh:

> What was from the beginning,
> what we have heard,
> what we have seen with our own eyes,
> what we have contemplated,
> what we have felt with our own hands
> of the Word of Life …
> what we have seen and heard,
> we announce to you,
> so that you may share life with us …
> and we write this in order that our Joy
> may be complete. (1 Jn 1: 1–4)

LIFE TO THE FULL

> "Thou Shalt Know Him When He Comes
> Not by any din of drums
> Nor the vantage of his airs
> Nor by anything he wears
> Neither by his crown
> Nor his gown.
>
> For His Presence Known Shall be
> By the Holy Harmony
> That His coming makes in thee."

(Unknown fifteenth-century writer)

A poet, writing centuries ago, summed up in one word what discernment eventually produces within us: *harmony*. The consolation that we savor at the end of the decision-making process is the evidence that we have reached an agreement with ourselves and with God. When the practice of discernment becomes habitual, it is this kind of harmony we can expect to feel more and more often.

We are in harmony because the different parts of our being are more frequently reconciled, at peace, one. Our heavy-handed rationalization represses fewer of our feelings; we have, as a result, fewer irrational explosions. Our guts become less able to manipulate and enslave our thinking and so we no longer feel it necessary to keep our minds closed with stubborn and agressive assertions. We are gradually liberated from the inner conflicts that have torn us apart in the past or pushed us from one extreme to another in our behavior.

We are in harmony because, more often now, both our head and our heart are sensitive to our God, our values, our name, and our mission in any of life's events. With increasing freedom our head and heart together are more capable of managing a life according to Agape. No drum roll announces this "Holy Harmony" taking place in us because it is only gradually that our actions become well rooted in Life and Love, in the Spirit of Agape. Progressively, we become more at peace with ourselves because we are step-by-step more in rhythm with God's word within us, more trustfully walking with the Lord in a very unique and personal way. We are in harmony, we *are* harmony, for we choose more easily Love and Life and not Death.

When we experience this harmony we start to understand the truth of the statement made by Irenaeus of Lyons in the second century AD, "The Glory of God is the human being fully alive." This does not mean that we enjoy spectacular and overwhelming triumphant *transformations*: no "airs," no "crown," no "gown," even though that might happen sometimes for some people. What we do experience is a progressive *transfiguration*.

We are still the same person, weak and limited, but other people may more frequently see the force of Love passing through us and, once in a while, we may see it ourselves. Maybe we don't yet feel "fully alive," but more and more obviously the Life of Love cannot be constrained by us, the Life of Love irradiates most of our deeds. People "may see goodness in [our] acts and give glory to God." (Mt 5: 16)

The gradual healing of our relationship with ourselves leaves us less and less inclined to project our brokenness into our relationships with others. So, too, as members of a group (if we are all used to discerning personally), when we reach a communal decision, we also experience mutual harmony. As partners in the decision-making process we savor "gladness and harmony" for we have made a long journey together: we worked to find a *common* starting point and we eventually reached a *joint* decision by coming to an agreement about choosing the *same* means. We may have fought with one another along the way but now, having learned to be more at peace with ourselves, we are also at peace with each other.

In the process we have undergone many liberations, some of them painful: we have had to overcome apprehension about expressing ourselves, dread of exposing our vulnerability, reluctance to sharing as deeply as possible. By risking the experience of a period of disagreement, we have vanquished the fear of our divisions, the fear of each other, *the fear of the other, the fear of ourselves.* But our final harmony also results from the fact that we have slowly let God tune our hearts, guts, and voices to the same basic values, to the key in which the Spirit sings the melodies of Agape.

The prayer of Jesus is realized in us in this way, in us as individuals or as members of a group, "That they may be one." (Jn 17: 21–22) The harmony in which we take such delight brings us peace and sometimes gives us joy — a peace and "a joy no one can take" because we have attained what *we really want.*

VERY OFTEN THROUGH A DEATH

It is not by chance that Jesus talked about his gift of peace and joy in the context of his Passion. (Jn 14: 27; 16: 21–22) For it is true that the delight we taste at the end of discernment about a serious matter often has nothing to do with an easy and superficial happiness. The process has sometimes been an arduous journey. I have already described part of the difficulty earlier in this book, but now I want to mention some other aspects of choosing that make it a hard thing to do.

When we reach a junction of several roads on our journey, we must take one of them if we want to keep on going. The fact is that we can choose only one path and, by choosing, we lose the possibility of walking along the others. The most perfect discernment does not change this simple fact of life, and this is painful; there is a foretaste of death in every choice we make. We may also die to the past we are leaving behind, or to the old person we abandon for the new one we are called to be. This is why discernment may include moments of pain and struggle and even of agony. This anguish is not surprising if we remember that discernment may imply a death to intellectual solutions that are not appropriate for us right now, and a death to some affective motivations that won't be satisfied in this present context. We may have to die to beautiful dreams because they do not fit us today. We die to subtle protections or immediate satisfactions. In any decision, we die. But we do not die alone ....

It was during his last supper with his disciples that Jesus talked about his peace and joy; it was a farewell before he died. (Jn 14: 27; 15: 11) For us, too, a very important decision might be a farewell to people and places we have known. Even if we use a very effective method, choices entail the risk of losses.

The journey we make is very much like the one we undergo in our physical death: we die alone and not alone. We die alone in the sense that each choice is our personal responsibility and our way, where nobody, even our closest friends, can follow. (Jn 13: 36) But, in another sense, we do not die alone because our choices affect our friends and the ripples reach other people. Each decision is a call for a Passover and an Exodus for everyone it touches: we are all leaving our old place for a new and unknown land, dying in order to be born anew. (Ex 14; Jos 1)

But when "the hour has come," we have to go, keeping in mind Jesus' words, "If the grain of wheat dies, it produces much fruit." (Jn 12: 23–24) Death is never the last word, "death is swallowed up in victory," in Jesus' victory. (1 Co 15: 54) If a decision leads us all to such a Passover, let us hope that "if we have been united with him through likeness to his death, so shall we be through a like resurrection." (Rom 6: 5)

"ALL SHALL BE WELL"

Painful or not, any decision made after a serious discernment opens onto a new life. And if the prospect of that new life gives us a feeling of harmony, it is because it fits us and the call of the Spirit at the deepest level of our being. It is *what we, both we and the Spirit, really want.* For our utmost desire, ours and God's, is our *well-being.*

Here is the experience of a friend of mine. She told me this:

One of my preoccupations in those days was finding God's will. I would say to myself, "If I found God's will and did it, I would have peace and all would be well." But the very idea of God's will terrified me because I was certain that it would demand a dreadful sacrifice, one I could never accept.

I remember a Friday evening, while relaxing on my bed, I was mulling over the problem of God's will. "God's will is our salvation" was the phrase bothering me. I had looked up the word salvation in Scripture: it meant well-being. Substituting the words "God's will is our well-being," it suddenly dawned on me (in the way that you unexpectedly see where a puzzle piece fits) God's will is my well-being. The deepest desire of God, the striving of God is toward my well-being. So, I don't have to struggle down here in me all my life to come up with something that fits in with God's arbitrary plan out there above — with the anguish that this might not fit me. This came as a shock to me! God wanted my well-being? This was not at all the God I had imagined. At that precise moment I became aware of someone: a presence in time of space, not seen, not heard, but utterly immanent ... and in the attitude of a petitioner ....

This testimony reveals a fairly common outlook on life. Many times we act as if we believed that if we accomplish God's will, we earn our well-being *from the outside,* both "vertically" and "horizontally." We earn it "vertically" when we feel peace, for instance, within us because we have done the will of Someone living *somewhere else* — in Heaven *above.* We earn it "horizontally," on the other hand, because our well-being is seen as a reward given *after* we have done God's will: "Do this and *then* you will have peace." When we view it this way, we imagine a *distance* between God's will and our well-being: distance in space (above us versus within us) and distance in time (between the moment we act and the moment of the reward that follows, the before and the after of our action). Such exteriority between God's will and our well-being explains our anguish: any reward, any will about us determined by an outsider, without our participation, might not fit us, might be a threat to the ones we are. That's what we find in my friend's account.

This book, on the contrary, shows that discernment, made carefully, destroys both the distance and the anguish at the end of the process (even though, as we have said, the pursuit of my well-being might lead me through a painful Passover, far beyond my false dreams, delusions, masks, idols, and noble ambitions). A serious discernment that leads me to *what we really want, both God and me, within myself,* abolishes the vertical distance. God's will is my will in the core of my being. And it removes the horizontal distance as well. At the same moment that I say "yes" to what I really want, consolation, peace, and harmony occur;

I experience myself as being well. Such feelings usually do not disappear when the decision is put into action, even if it is a hard one to act on, for consolation strengthens us.

The author of Genesis illustrates that God's will and desire is our well-being by painting a picture of Adam and Eve. Before they choose to depart from their real welfare, they are living in harmony in the Garden of Eden with nature, animals, each other, and the Creator. (Gn 2–3) The original intention of God is, therefore, clear for the writer of that mythical story: that "all shall be well." (Julian of Norwich) And all of the Old Testament, by evoking the nostalgia of the human being before the wound, reminds us that Israel has clung to the belief that God always does everything possible to heal, forgive, and save humankind.

Jesus belongs to this tradition. When he feeds the crowds, it is very abundantly. (Mt 14: 20; 15: 37) When he is present at a wedding he supplies the celebrants with plenty of the most delicious wine. (Jn 2) When he heals or forgives, he gives people back their well-being. He is the Good Shepherd with whom all "shall not want." (Ps 23) All his deeds confirm his words, "I come that they might have life and have it to the full." (Jn 10: 10)

God's desire for our well-being is so passionate that nothing can stop it. It is shown by the end of my friend's narrative:

> The attitude of this Holy petitioner was so exquisitely gentle and nonintrusive that I could not be afraid. I got up immediately, I did not hesitate to say "Yes." For a long time I was wholly absorbed in that presence and completely lost to myself.
>
> Afterward, trying to interpret, I gave words to the petition. It was really an appeal. Someone disarmingly humble and unassuming was asking permission, "May I use anything? …" Now I was frustrated! I had said "yes" without hearing the rest of the question. But it seemed to me it was this: "Will you let me use anything … everything… for your well-being?"

It was an artist-spirit, the creative spirit that emerged from the shadows that evening, the One for whom nothing is useless, nothing is discarded; everything, no matter how damaged, it redeemable.

I had totally misunderstood God.

Perhaps the best example of this conception of God comes to us in the Christian tradition. For our well-being, God used a tremendous human tragedy born from events, the crucifixion of Jesus, and changed it into the instrument of our salvation. The way of the cross became, by the force of God's desire for our well-being, the way of redemption. And God keeps doing this for us; with a "power at work in us" the Lord does "immeasurably more than we ask or imagine," and uses everything brought to us by life and makes it a grace for our well-being. (Ep 3: 20–21) Borrowing the words of the Curé de Campagne of Bernanos (*Diary of a Country Priest*) that echo Paul's in Romans 8, we can say, "Everything is grace," even the Passovers we face in our discernments.

Our daily challenge is this: whether our decisions are big ones or small ones (selecting a menu, moving, finding a new job, getting married, remaining single, accepting a ministry, choosing a school for our children, starting a business, etc.), we have to discern, distinguish accurately with the Spirit of Agape, where Life and Love, our real well-being might be for us. God wants our well-being and calls us for that everywhere and at all times. Love around us and Love within us seeks us out in the most hidden or public lives, just as Love sought Jesus in Nazareth and in Jerusalem. Love expects us in the most pleasant and difficult places, as Love expected Jesus in Cana and on Golgotha.

When we first start practicing discernment, we suppose that *we* are searching for God; when we get used to discerning we discover that, in each decision, God was there searching for us, giving us a *rendezvous* at the core of our being. God's will is to meet us, to be and stay with us in any circumstances of our life. And when our discernment is done, when the full recognition, decision, and encounter take place, there is our well-being, Agape, revealed in our depth, as God-with-us, Emmanuel.

In all our discernments, we repeat the words of the Bride, "Have you seen Him whom my heart loves?" But all along the way our very search has been a response to the Spirit whispering in our depth, through any event, "Come now, my love." (Sg 2–3)

Always Unfinished: A Grace

The story of the Bride of the Canticle of Canticles reminds us that our relationship with God is a love story, where we are "lost and found" again and again. (Lk 15: 32) The quest, and then the necessity of discernment, is never finished before we die. As long as we are here on earth we are on our way, choosing our road, for a trip that is *unfinished.*

It is unfinished first within us. Our inner harmony never reaches perfection. It is true that some of our wounds can be healed, but some will become more or less sensitive scars, and some will remain as wounds. The intention of this book was to suggest that the most important thing for each one of us is to be aware of them and able to manage our life with this knowledge and to make decisions for Life and Love, our well-being.

Our journey is unfinished in another sense. Most of us can expect to see a few tomorrows, and so, we can assume that we'll face again many choices, and therefore many discernments — and further Passovers ... until the last one, our physical death. We are never perfectly healed and never perfectly settled down until we cross the final Red Sea and enter the Promised Land, experiencing the perfect liberation by and in God. Right now, everything and everybody is unfinished.

We do not like that because we easily forget that we are nomads — Jews, Christians, or Moslems, all heirs of the Hebrew tribes and their God. However, the unfinished quality of our lives is a blessing. It assures that, if nothing can be perfectly accomplished for and by us here and now, nothing can be definitively lost or missed, nothing is totally irreparable — unfinished means that no death is a dead end. Being unfinished is a grace: it is a mercy for us when we fail in our choices, it is a challenge for us to make "one more step ahead" through each decision. The word *unfinished* suggests infinite. It is a call to a road never closed and barred, a road wide open to life, to everlasting life. It is for us an invitation to learn the fathomless melodies of Agape within us and to compose, like Schubert, our own "Unfinished Symphony," step by step, choice after choice,

> Day by day, dear Lord,
> of Thee three things I pray.
> To see Thee more clearly,
> Love Thee more dearly,
> Follow Thee more nearly,
> Day by day.
> > *Richard of Chichester*
> > c. 1197–1253

Appendix 1
More about the Four Criteria

In workshops on discernment that I have facilitated, various groups have felt the necessity to explore the content of the four criteria more systematically than I have done in the chapter of this book concerning *How to Work with My Head*. Here is what those people added:

First Criterion:
TO BE ROOTED, GROUNDED (Incarnation)

—— To take myself as I am and not as I dream of being: to accept my body (my size, my face, my man- or womanhood, my health); my mind (sharp, slow, intelligent, imaginative); my sense of organization; my capacity to perceive what is important, my tendency to get lost in details; my heart (sensitive, vulnerable, shy, guarded, loving, compassionate, afraid); my heredity, education, training, past experiences, values; to be the one I am without mask or without trying to play a role — objectively and realistically to be the one I am.

—— To take others as they are and not as I would like them to be: to accept and respect their bodies, minds, hearts; where they come from, where they are now instead of where I want them to be; their ideas, opinions, reactions, past, culture, aspirations, dreams.

—— To take facts as they are: to look at the real situation as it is, without prejudices and, if possible, unemotionally, with objectivity.

—— To collect basic information and to make a serious analysis of the situation, utilizing experts or research; to act like a third party, a qualified one, to try to reach intellectual honesty.

—— To accept the "here and now"; this place, this time, and not elsewhere; to accept the ambiguities of human life with its ups and downs, never perfectly black or white; not to dream (in the bad sense of the word) but to see what is possible right now.

Second Criterion:
TO GIVE , TO BE GIVEN UP

—— To give: my smile, my knowledge, my friendship, my competence, my time, my money, my joy, my compassion, my understanding, my care.

—— To be given up: to let others ask for and take something that is a part of me (my time, my knowledge, my availability); to let them use me (in my family circle, my coworkers); to give up, when necessary, my tranquility, my gain, my prejudices, my opinions, my control, my power, to the point of vulnerability and powerlessness.

—— To listen to the ones who know more than I do; to delegate, to depend on, to allow freedom, not to insist on doing everything by myself; to let people grow up, learn, make mistakes, take initiative.

Third Criterion:
UNIVERSALITY

—— To remember that we always belong to several wholes, that we are at their intersection; so, to try to take them all into consideration without neglecting any of them.

—— To be tolerant, to welcome, to be open to others' ideas, words, projects — even when they contradict my own; to value others' suggestions; to improve my ways of relating with the other gender, generations, countries, cultures, religions; to be ready to change, to modify my point of view; faced with criticism, to try to extract what may be true in it.

—— Not to ignore a sector of my life: to take into account my body and my mind and my heart; my spouse and my children and my friends; my acquaintances and my business and my leisure; my political and social and religious life; my department, my firm, my city, my state, my nation, the world. To keep the same idea in my mind concerning others: they belong to several wholes too, and they have the right to take all of them into account.

—— To oppose any discrimination (because of gender, age, social milieu, race, color, creed, education); to refuse to adopt a "ghetto" mentality.

—— In each situation, to consider what would be the step toward more universality: for instance, if I am very concerned about my own department, can I try to be a little more concerned about my firm; although I have no problem being involved in my family life, am I ignoring my neighborhood?

Fourth Criterion:
TO BE PART OF, TO WEAVE (Communion)

—— To oppose indifference, divisions, rejections; to admit differences but to be a builder of bridges between myself and others, between people; not to play someone against somebody else; to be a witness and instrument of forgiveness and reconciliation; to weave and reweave without despair.

—— To share and to invite people to share what may be shared; to be concerned about the ones who are not enjoying their human rights and to act on their behalf; to do what I can everywhere to involve the forgotten, the excluded, the rejected, the neediest ones.

Appendix 2

Is This Method Only for Christians?

How can people without Christian faith make this method their own? Everybody has a head and a heart, follows values, and makes decisions. So non-Christians and nonbelievers can use the content of this book. And Christians, more easily than might be believed, can practice discernment for a common decision, using this method, with people who do not share their faith. The one problem that must be solved is to translate the four criteria into words appropriate to the language and values of the ones who are not Christian. This is not too difficult. I have done that with some Jewish and nonbelieving friends. Let me tell you briefly the translation we worked out for both of these points of view.

A JEWISH TRANSLATION OF THE FOUR CRITERIA

INCARNATION

The first criterion grows out of the very root of Jewish faith. God's love for the Hebrews was manifested, not in a general and vague way, but through very *particular* — incarnate— signs. It was a unique choice with a distinct people in a specific time and a special land. There are also many very *concrete* prescriptions of the Law (613 for some Jews) that invite the People of God to prove their love through incarnate ways.

TO GIVE, TO BE GIVEN UP

The second criterion is founded on the many *gifts* showing God's love for the Chosen People: the Covenant, the Law, and the Promised Land. "I gave you a land which you had not tilled and cities you had not built, to dwell in. You have eaten of vineyards and olive groves which you did not plant," says the Lord. (Jos 24: 13) Such gratuitous love calls Jews to act in the same way, even toward the foreigner. (Dt 24: 17–18)

Jews are called *to be given up* to God, as God-Adonai was given up to them. God-Adonai's credibility was handed over to the Jews in the sense that, depending on their witness, the Nations would be able to know the Lord. The Holy One of Israel never revoked this abandonment to their behavior. (Ez 36: 20–22)

UNIVERSALITY

Because of love, God chose and blessed Abraham, but that choice and blessing was aimed at *all* Nations. (Gn 12: 3) The writer of Genesis extended that favor to all humankind through Noah, and the prophets reiterated God's grace for all people. (Gn 9: 9; Is 45; 56; Ps 87; 98) How could the Jews refuse to be universal, faced with the Lord's words, "I come to gather nations of every language. They shall come and see my glory." (Is 66: 18) This world view is not the only aspect of universality; holism is also a part of it. How can Jews forget any part of themselves when God's dealings with them had been at the level of all their most concrete concerns. No sector of human life is ignored in the Scriptures. It is there that we spotted the third criterion.

COMMUNION

Finally, we saw the last criterion in the whole history of Israel. Continually marked by a specificity that maintains distinction, that history always calls for *union*. It is the history of a communion unceasingly threatened and renewed. Between man and woman, for example, among twelve tribes becoming one single People; among Jews invited to celebrate henceforth in one single Temple; for Jewish deportees brought back from the Exile to the same homeland; between Israel and the Nations; for it is the history of God's fidelity to *a covenant with sinful human beings*. (Gn 2–3)

Again keeping the four criteria together as a fifth criterion, God's faithfulness to the descendants of Adam and Eve through Israel has always been a whole; since God's love cannot be cut into slices, the Jews cannot ignore any of the criteria in a discernment.

A Translation of the Four Criteria for Nonbelievers

INCARNATION

With people who have no belief in God or in an afterlife, the first criterion arises from the fact that we have only one life to live. So, if we want to live, it is necessary to be as available as possible in the present moment to the persons we are with, and as the persons we are at this precise time. Death always ready to knock at our door reminds us not to waste our time in meaningless dreams, but to incarnate our love *here and now* — our feet on the ground, for we won't get another chance.

TO GIVE, TO BE GIVEN UP

For many nonbelievers those two expressions summarize love. Accordingly, it is logical for them to *give* everything possible to improve the human condition. Convinced of the uniqueness of human beings, they fight against injustice, oppression, and suffering affecting anyone. Many also, aware that giving might still imply a kind of selfish control on their part, have discovered the value and the need to accept *to be given up* to other social classes, cultures, and countries in order to serve them with a more altruistic love. Books like *The Art of Loving*, by Erich Fromm, demonstrate that nonbelievers can plumb the depths of love.

UNIVERSALITY

It is not necessary to have any religious faith to believe that *all* human beings are equal and deserve the same respect without discrimination. The scientific works of the UN after World War II that refuted the Nazi rationalization for racism; the United Nations Declaration of Human Rights; the philosophy of the World Health Organization, of the International Labor Organization, UNESCO, and UNICEF have proven that. Universality is the reality of the day: each one's world is the whole world. To love with a provincial love is to accept to be amputated from our worldly body.

COMMUNION

The fourth criterion can be summed up with the word *solidarity*. More and more we grow together. If one of us hurts, the others cannot be happy. The universal risk of nuclear weapons and the pollution of the earth, the bonds created by our current media and the scientific community, the economic interconnections and dependency between countries have taught us that we are intertwined with one another. What happens at one end of this world concerns everybody everywhere else. We see that in the discovery of penicillin in the USA, in the 1978 oil crisis, in the invention of radio and television, in the East Europe revolutions, in the manufacturing of electronic chips, in Chernobyl in Russia, in the green revolution, in Black Monday on Wall Street in October 1987, etc. We cannot ignore the world for we are already all in communion. The media brings to our living room the joys and the sufferings, the pleas of misery as well as the celebrations of our whole city, nation, and planet. More and more we become *one* world; if we claim that we want to love, we embrace with an enlarged heart all our brothers and sisters, all human beings.

As for the fifth criterion, let us say that the four criteria are like concentric inseparable circles. The whole crumbles if one of them is neglected. For instance, a true solidarity implies the acceptance of all; but that universal love supposes people giving and being given up; and that would be just words if it were not concretely put into practice, incarnate.

Therefore, once translated, the four criteria can be used by anybody who wants to discern where love is calling for action. That is not a surprise because everyone has a head and a heart. Love is not owned by Christians; all human beings, with or without religious belief, can love.

Translation of the Chapter How to Listen to My Heart for People Who Are Not Christian

Non-Christians and nonbelievers can easily translate this chapter. It is sufficient to say this: people only have to let their intellectual solution sink into the deepest levels of their affectivity and to listen to the echoes sent back to their conscious level by their guts. That is already implied in the common sense question we often ask each other, "How do you feel about that?" "Stifling" feelings will say to the ones who are discerning that the solution they envision is not welcomed by their inner being, because it is, very probably, dangerous for them. "Enlivening" feelings, on the contrary, will assert that the solution elaborated by their head is approved by their deepest self. In any case, my statements are rooted in the awareness that we all have that, at a very profound level within ourselves, we know, somehow, what might hurt us or nurture our life. Even our bodies know if a grafted organ fits them, and they are able to reject the ones that do not belong.

Appendix 3

What Can We Do to Clarify the Object of the Choice?

What can I do when I have a nagging feeling that there is a choice to be made but I have difficulty "hearing the exact words" of the question? I may know, for example, that it revolves around the issue of the poor, or an attraction to working in Latin America, or the fact that "I can't say no" to people, or a vague uneasiness about my job, but it is not clear.

Before doing anything else it is necessary to work on listening to the question within me. Sometimes eliminating is an efficient means, "No, it is not concerning my relationship with my husband; No, it does not deal with my job; etc."

But, if after reflection, I still find myself saying, "I don't know exactly what's the matter," and I cannot express in positive terms the question, "Yes, it has to do with moving; Indeed, it's about wasting money; etc." it would be better to forget trying to make a decision. Let us put the question aside. But if I still have no peace, I may have to take some systematic steps in order to coax the exact nature of the choice to emerge from the shadows.

First, I must respect my need for *time*. I take my time: this requires being patient with my lack of clarity. Suffering it means that I'll resist internal and external pressure to "come up with" something that resembles a decision. Also I *give* my time to it: I schedule moments for reflecting, pondering, musing, and mulling it over. I include reading about the general subject of my ponderings and using other ways of gathering information about it, if necessary. I pray, asking for the grace of clarification.

Second, it might be very helpful to find someone who can listen to me as I try to come to grips with the nature of my problem — a person with no need to advise, who is a good listener. Someone who facilitates clarification by giving me honest feedback about my clarity or lack of it, who knows how to ask clarifying questions: "Do you mean that you don't feel your present job is giving you a chance to use your problem-solving skills?" — "It's not clear to me what's bothering you about your marriage." — "What do you mean by 'the poor'?" It's up to me to see if I need a professional listener for that purpose.

A third step in helping ourselves to begin to articulate a vague and formless question is to touch the general area, to establish contact. Suppose I am pestered by the presence of the poor in my consciousness: I might volunteer my services on a regular basis and for a while with an agency based in the slums and see what clarification develops; I might do the same by volunteering my presence to prisoners, handicapped people, the elderly, etc. If I have been toying with the idea of adoption, for example, I might decide to provide foster care to a child for a period of time to get a feel for what this would mean for our family life and me. If the idea of divorce is menacing in the distance, I might want to embark on a temporary separation.

Appendix 4

Dealing with a Spiritual Helper

In all religions, people have gone to persons particularly aware about spiritual matters in order to be helped, and very often when it was time for making decisions. When we do so, it would be better to avoid someone who is unqualified or who is going to exploit us. So, how can we recognize a good spiritual helper? This note gives some brief advice about that question.

The names that have been given in Christianity to "gurus" already warn us about possible risks. We spoke of spiritual father, director, guide, master, or counselor.

Father, director, guide, master might suggest that the helper knows everything, and even our own road; therefore, we might let him or her give us orders and childishly submit ourselves to the helper's commands. That will never develop our sense of self-efficacy and personal responsibility. (Let us remember, however, that the goal of an authentic father or master is to promote the growth of the children or disciples toward autonomy; the hope is that one day they will be parents or masters themselves.) *Counselor* seems better, so long as it implies help for better self-expression and awareness, giving advice but never orders and avoiding personal projections. But, sometimes our sessions with spiritual counselors are only counseling; we starve for spiritual food for we are journeying toward someone who is God.

I must emphasize that these names have very often been associated with men only, even though, despite this tendency in our Christian past, history abounds with examples of women who have been very accurate spiritual experts for everybody. I would like to point out that, in the description I will give of the role and character of the spiritual helper, I have clearly in my mind women as well as men, lay persons as well as the ordained.

That is why I like to join people who use the word *accompanist* to describe this role. This expression means that even though the helper walks with us, the road is ours; that while the accompanist plays a musical instrument, it is supporting a song that is our own. The chords played by the accompanist can reinforce our song and might make all its potentialities resound. As long as we are aware of the risks of such a relationship for both of us, the name does not matter too much.

IS THE SPIRITUAL ACCOMPANIST A PSYCHOTHERAPIST?

Using the word *counselor* we implied that it would be useful for the accompanist to know about psychology. That raises the question, "Is spiritual help psychotherapy?" On one hand, it is true that during our meetings with our helper we sometimes go back to our childhood (and it is impossible to grow spiritually while ignoring our past), but on the other hand there is an essential difference between the two processes.

In some methods of psychotherapy, through some exercises (dreams, group process, and others) the clients talk about their lives. The therapist responds according to the school he or she follows, frequently sending the clients back to childhood. The hope is that through such a journey certain events of the past come back to memory with their real impact revealed, and that the clients will be more able to decode their current behaviors and make better decisions. Freed from their subconscious motivations, they'll manage their lives in a happier way. For, since Freud, many methods of psychotherapy are based on the belief that our subconscious motivations drive us to pursue a well-being by ways that are not effective.

The therapist sends the clients to their childhood *by themselves, alone.*

The spiritual accompanist, using methods and exercises (meditation, contemplation, centering prayer, and others), apparently does the same work. For self-discovery always involves the discovery of our childhood and its wounds. But the spiritual helper does not send us back to that time by ourselves, but *with the Spirit of God.* For the relationship of the partners in this process is based on faith, the helper's and ours. When the two persons are Christians, they believe that human beings are indwelt by the Spirit of Jesus Christ, the Risen One.

Our faith does not change our memories with the emotions they trigger, but it does give us a greater courage for making the trip back in time. We walk through our childhood with the certainty that Someone accompanies us. We pass through water and fire with the strength of the Spirit of God. (Is 43: 1–5) We touch our wounds with the compassion of the Real Good Samaritan. (Lk 10: 25–37) We face our mistakes with the forgiveness of Jesus. (Is 1: 18) Victorious, we enter a new life through new decisions with the Spirit of Christ, who conquered sin and death. We know we have been always loved and, with that faith, everything becomes possible. (Jer 31: 31)

In fact, the spiritual accompanist sends us back to the Spirit of God within ourselves. The Spirit reveals and treats any wounds that might still be at the roots of our captivity. (Lk 4: 18) Taught by the Spirit of Life and Agape, we learn how to decode our behaviors and manage ourselves more consciously. Our choices are made with the Spirit. We become freer and happier, as human beings and believers. Let us now examine qualities we should look for in a good accompanist.

Conscious of Being an Intruder

When we talk to our spiritual helper, it is better to share everything in our life, for everything is spiritual: God cherishes our whole life, inhabits us wherever we are and whatever we do, calls us in any situation. We share everything because everything is a place for an annunciation and incarnation. Men or women, as single or married persons, as children or parents, as workers or citizens, God always says to us the words Mary heard, "As Agape, I want to be present and incarnate in this world through you, through your flesh. What is your decision?" (Lk 1: 26–38)

There is no law that says we must share everything. But it is a necessity if we don't want to miss these announcements, and if we want to see their incarnation accomplished when we say, "I am the servant of the Lord." Therefore, our sessions with our accompanist often deal with our most intimate and confidential issues. That is why spiritual helpers must always remember that they are in a sense intruders, in spite of the liberty we allow them. And even more when it is time for us to make a decision that belongs to our responsibility.

They are guests invited to our banquet with the Lord, so they must "grow less" like John the Baptist when bridegroom and bride come together, they must "make (their) way to the lowest place and sit there" according to Jesus' word. (Jn 3: 29–30; Lk 14: 10) Let us say that they can never be tactful enough, they can never be respectful and delicate enough. This does not mean that they don't have to do anything; but before describing their role, what other qualities do we need to find in good accompanists?

A Charism

Spiritual helpers have a kind of charism. (1 Co 12: 10) But sometimes we forget to check out if this gift is really there. We have already given two signs of the presence of that charism, respect and delicacy. Let us see in what these qualities are rooted.

A PERSONAL SPIRITUAL EXPERIENCE

Authentic accompanists speak from their own experience. They may well have studied about spiritual matters — and that is all to the good — but their wisdom does not come from books alone, but essentially from their personal experience.

If they are respectful and delicate with us it is because they themselves have experienced, in their own ways, sin and temptation, guilt and contrition, dryness and consolation, doubt and certainty, anger and mercy, hatred and love. If they can help us it is because they too have been attacked by perfectionism and exaggerated asceticism, they too have been vulnerable to fear and weakness in adversity, they too have been charmed by Agape. And they too have struggled for making choices.

Having made their own journey with its joys and sorrows, they cannot be surprised or scandalized by our reactions, they cannot be other than delicate for they know firsthand what it means to be a frail and sinful human being. Having walked with God, they are respectful with us for they know themselves the mysteries and the price of the Exodus, the value of the answer, "Yes, here I am Lord." The accompanist knows well that what we are dealing with and sharing is at once intimate and unfathomable.

SPIRITUAL SENSITIVITY

All people have had spiritual experiences in their lives; however, not all of us have the grace of spiritual penetration and the talent of articulating our insights to help others. (1 Co 12: 8) This gift is favored by intuition with which we are able to detect the calls of Life and the threats of Death in any area of our existence.

—— "I am devastated for my best friend has cancer!" said someone to his accompanist. At the end of a lengthy conversation in which he could express his tumultuous feelings, he heard his spiritual helper replying, "Yes, it is terrible ... is it not also for you a call to love her more right now?" His image of the event, though still awful, was altered.

—— "My boss congratulated me for what I had done. Strangely, I could not handle her congratulations," complained a factory worker. In the process of dialogue, he got back in touch with the question of his self-image ... so the accompanist could say, "Are you discounting yourself ... are you not God's son?"

Usually we are struck by good accompanists' interpretations. Deep down within ourselves we feel the words hit the target. Whether it concerns our family, social, or political life, we find that our helper has touched the right spot, and this is helpful for discernment. Neither training nor ordination can guarantee such intuition, it is a charism.

SKILL IN LISTENING

We might guess that good spiritual helpers are skillful listeners. Remaining silent for a while before reacting, refraining from personal projections like an affective counselor, caring like a friend are excellent behaviors, but something else is necessary. Accompanists try to perceive what might be revealed within us; their real question is, "*Behind the words I hear, beyond the events narrated, what is going on in terms of temptations or invitations, in terms of fascination by Death or calls from Agape?*" Answering these questions clarifies the alternatives of a choice.

That explains why they don't act as judges or moralists, why they cannot break the "bruised reed" we are, because their goal is not our virtue or our perfection. (Is 42: 3) Faith is the level at which they work, remembering Kierkegaard's statement, "In the Gospel, the opposite of sin is never virtue, but faith." Crippled with the crippled, lame with the lame, sinful men or women, they try to discern with us the "one more step ahead" we can make in our current situation in order to answer —— as faith-ful (1), the present call to the banquet of the Savior. (Ez 33: 11; Jn 10: 10; Lk 14: 21; Mt 9: 13)

CAPACITY FOR NAMING

A special aspect of the listening of the accompanists is *naming*. The spiritual helper tries to identify who we are by raising questions about our name, "Are you in your business David fighting against gigantic adversities, and needing to stand firm in your faith in God's strength?" (1 Sa 17) "In your social life do you feel abandoned by God like Zion and thirsty for the Lord's faithful presence?" (Is 49: 14–16) "Dealing with the outcast, are you Judas or Peter betraying or denying the Crucified One, and called to contrition?" (Lk 22: 48, 54–62) "In your political involvement are you Jeremiah crushed and mocked, doubting God's power against violence?" (Jer 15: 18–21) "With your spouse, are you Ruth or Mary, desiring to welcome love in your flesh and saying, 'Wherever you go, I shall go'?" (Ru 1: 16; Lk 1: 26–38) To know my "name" is already saying something about my "mission."

Then our spiritual helper, with respect and delicacy, suggests to us some "working hypotheses" about our current identity; and we discover which ones are accurate, through the emotions they create within us. So, *together with our accompanist*, we can eventually "name" clearly the son or the daughter of God we are right now. And, through a personal Revelation that is really ours, we can discover and accept our "mission." The birth of Jesus was announced to Mary and Joseph: when we seek spiritual help we are Mary (female or male) pregnant with new life; the accompanist cannot be more than Joseph (male or female) who participates in naming the child, the child who is ours and God's — for we are God's People. (Lk 1: 31; Mt 1: 21)

"LET MY PEOPLE GO ..."

Once we have been named, our accompanist must let us go. The discovered road is our own, and the Lord says, "Let my People go." (Ex 7: 16) And we go to the place where our personal covenant will be renewed and celebrated again. We must go and not cling to our helper either. What dependency or possessiveness hides there if neither of us can let go? Are we still slaves? Has our accompanist become our Pharaoh?

This is the sign of an authentic relationship with spiritual accompanists: *it is mutually freeing.* Spiritual help is not a one-way street. We both grow deeper in the knowledge of our susceptibility to Death and to the Spirit of Life and Love; so we can both become freer for serving others. (Ga 5: 1–13) This freedom gives Joy. We have been searching and now we savor the Joy of answering God's call. When true accompanists perceive us welcoming the Lord through our decision, that is sufficient for them. They are like the disciples of Jesus, who heard him say, "… and there will be gifts for you, pressed down, shaken together, and running over." (Mt 25: 1–10; Lk 6: 38) What they have seen and heard is so fulfilling that they easily accept taking up less space in the life of the one they help, and even to disappearing; they can exult, "My Joy is complete." (1 Jn 1: 1–4; Lk 2: 20; Jn 3: 30)

Appendix 5
Diagrams

PART ONE:
THE GENERAL STRUCTURE OF DISCERNMENT

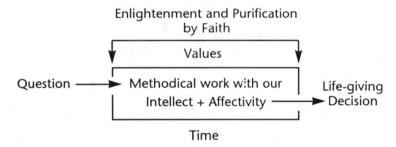

Enlightenment and Purification
by Faith

Values

Question ⟶ Methodical work with our
Intellect + Affectivity ⟶ Life-giving Decision

Time

PART TWO:
CHAPTER 1, HOW TO WORK WITH MY HEAD—THE FOUR CRITERIA

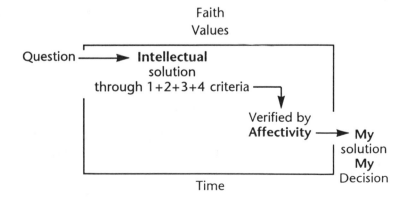

Faith
Values

Question ⟶ **Intellectual**
solution
through 1+2+3+4 criteria ⟶
Verified by
Affectivity ⟶ **My**
solution
My
Decision

Time

PART TWO:
CHAPTER 2, HOW TO LISTEN TO MY HEART

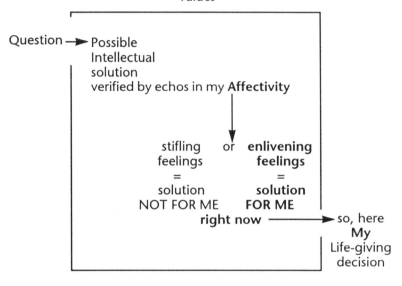

PART TWO:
CHAPTER 3, HOW TO BECOME
FREER FROM THE BEGINNING

Faith
Values

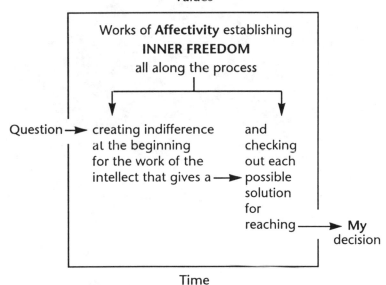

Time

Appendix 6
Index of Scriptures

The pages of the book are in parentheses.

36 *(70)*; 10: 34–36 *(54)*; 11: 12 *(54)*; 11: 15 *(96)*; 12:20 *(28)*; 13: 9 *(96)*; 13: 33*(27)*; 13: 43 *(96)*; 14: 20 *(115)*; 15: 24 *(25)*; 15: 37 *(115)*; 16: 13–23 *(52)*; 16: 17 *(95)*; 18: 19–20 *(80)*; 21: 31 *(28)*; 23: 37 *(25)*; 24: 4–5 *(29)*; 25: 1–10 *(138)*; 25: 31–46 *(8, 108)*; 26: 45–46 *(70)*

Mark 1: 11 *(34)*; 7: 31–37 *(96)*; 9: 23 *(72)*; 10:22 *(47)*; 10: 32–40 *(48)*

Luke 1: 26–38 *(134, 137)*; 1: 31 *(137)*; 1: 39–55 *(86)*; 1: 76 *(86)*; 2: 20 *(138)*; 2: 40–52 *(27, 34)*; 4: 18 *(133)*; 6: 38 *(138)*; 6: 43, 45 *(45)*; 9: 51–56 *(92)*; 10: 25–37 *(41, 108, 133)*; 12: 54–56 *(107)*; 14: 10 *(134)*; 14: 21 *(136)*; 15: 32 *(117)*; 16: 10 *(28, 67)*; 17: 10 *(86)*; 22: 24–27 *(95)*; 22: 48, 54–62 *(137)*

John 1: 14 *(23)*; 1: 38 *(ix)*; 2 *(115)*; 3: 8 *(107)*; 3: 29–30 *(134, 138)*; 5: 17 *(72)*; 7: 11–13, 40–44 *(25)*; 8: 7 *(86)*; 8: 36 *(95)*; 8: 44 *(51)*; 10: 10 *(41, 115, 136)* 11: 51 *(22)*; 12: 23–24 *(113)*; 13: 1 *(24)*; 13: 36 *(112)*; 14: 27 *(97, 112)*; 15: 2 *(47)*; 15: 10–11 *(97, 112)*; 16: 21–22 *(112)*; 17: 21–22 *(97, 111)*

Acts *(25, 88)*; 2 *(88)*; 9 *(50)*; 15 *(97)*; 15: 28 *(94)*; 15: 36–40 *(92)*; 17: 25, 28 *(41)*; 19 *(89)*; 22 *(50)*; 26 *(50)*

Romans 5: 6 *(40)*; 5: 12–19 *(40, 50)*; 6: 5 *(113)*; 7: 5 *(40)*; 8 *(116)*; 8: 5–6 *(40)*; 8: 11 *(48)*; 8: 13 *(40, 47)*; 8: 16 *(40, 43, 69)*; 8: 26–27 *(40, 107)*; 12: 2 *(10)*

1 Corinthians 1: 4–9 *(72)*; 1: 21 *(96)*; 2: 2 *(96)*; 2: 11–12 *(33)*; 3: 16 *(25)*; 10: 13 *(72)*; 12: 7 *(94)*; 12: 8 *(135)*; 12: 10 *(134)*; 13 *(30)*; 15: 54 *(113)*

2 Corinthians 1: 18 *(26)*

Galatians 1: 11–24 *(14)*; 1: 13–14 *(50)*; 3: 28 *(24)*; 5: 1–13 *(138)*; 5: 22–23 *(39)*

Ephesians 1: 5*(69)*; 3: 20–21 *(116)*; 5: 10 *(44)*

Philippians 1: 9–10 *(22)*; 2: 5–11 *(22, 23)*; 4: 13 *(72)*

Colossians *(63)*

1 Timothy 1: 13 *(50)*

1 John 1: 1–4 *(109, 138)*; 4: 1 *(45)*; 4: 8 *(10)*

Revelation 2 *(95)*

Suggested Readings

There are not too many books that treat specifically Ignatius' method of discernment. However, these publications are valuable.

Green, Thomas H., S. J. *Weeds Among the Wheat.* Discernment: Where Prayer and Action Meet. Notre Dame, IN: Ave Maria Press, 1983.

English, John J., S. J. *Spiritual Freedom.* From an experience of the Ignatian exercises to the art of spiritual direction. Guelph, Ontario: Loyola House, 1982.

Studies in the Spirituality of Jesuits, published by the American Assistancy Seminar on Jesuit Spirituality, Fusz Memorial, Saint Louis University, 3700 West Pine Blvd., Saint Louis, Missouri:

—— Futrell, John Carroll, S.J., "Ignatian Discernment." Volume VI, n. 4, June 1974.

—— Orsy, Ladislas, S.J., "Toward a Theological Evaluation of Communal Discernment." Volume V, n. 5, October 1973.